Jean Sabatine, a leader in the fields of movement for actors and jazz dance, is a professor of dramatic arts and head of the dance and movement program in the Department of Dramatic Arts at the University of Connecticut. She is also the founder, director, and choreographer of Jazz Dance Theatre and has done extensive choreography for both musical theatre and for the concert stage. The author of a book on jazz dance and several articles, she has conducted numerous workshops in theatre dance forms and stage movement around the country.

A member of the Screen Actor's Guild and Actor's Equity, **David Hodge** is a professional actor who has had extensive experience performing musical comedy, contemporary drama, and classical productions primarily in regional theatre. An M.F.A. graduate from Pennsylvania State University, he has taught acting, jazz dance, and movement for the actor in university and private sectors.

Prentice-Hall International, Inc., *London*
Prentice-Hall of Australia Pty. Limited, *Sydney*
Prentice-Hall Canada Inc., *Toronto*
Prentice-Hall of India Private Limited, *New Delhi*
Prentice-Hall of Japan, Inc., *Tokyo*
Prentice-Hall of Southeast Asia Pte. Ltd., *Singapore*
Whitehall Books Limited, *Wellington, New Zealand*
Editora Prentice-Hall do Brasil Ltda., *Rio de Janeiro*

The Actor's Image

Movement Training for Stage and Screen

Jean Sabatine

In collaboration with David Hodge

A SPECTRUM BOOK

Prentice-Hall, Inc., Englewood Cliffs, New Jersey 07632

Library of Congress Cataloging in Publication Data

Sabatine, Jean.
   The actor's image.

   "A Spectrum Book."
   Bibliography: p.
   Discography: p.
   Includes index.
     1. Movement (Acting)   I. Hodge, David (David G.)
II. Title.
PN2071.M6S2 1983   792'.028   83-9778
ISBN 0-13-003889-X
ISBN 0-13-003871-7 (pbk.)

*To my students—with your talent, commitment, and creativity,
I have discovered and perfected the tools that I use to help those
who have come after you.*

*Your collaboration with me would never have been
possible, however, without the support and education provided
by my parents, Frank and Jane Sabatine. To them I owe
all the honor and dedication that I have received from you.*

10 9 8 7 6 5 4 3 2 1

ISBN 0-13-003889-X

ISBN 0-13-003871-7 {PBK.}

Editorial/production supervision by Rita Young
Manufacturing buyers: Christine Johnston and Edward J. Ellis
Cover design by Hal Siegel

CONTENTS

FOREWORD

The Actor's Image: Movement Training for Stage and Screen fills an aching void in actor training literature and movement writing in general. This book unites the three primary disciplines of acting—acting, voice, and movement.

Two of the most essential and often most elusive of an actor's tools are focus and energy. No artist can improve the quality of his craft if he is lacking in these basics. Ms. Sabatine provides a streamlined process whereby the actor can improve his physical, mental, and spiritual concentration, which in turn results in breeding energy. There is a rationale to the system here devised and the author skillfully guides the artist through each section of study. It is a pathway to clarity and energy. Once the route is learned the actor need never be lost again in his journey to better his craft.

In her successfully developed theory, an actor is provided with a step-by-step process for dealing with characterizations in a variety of theatrical images and character types. While many of the techniques described by Ms. Sabatine will be familiar to the trained actor, the chief strength of *The Actor's Image* is that it builds upon the foundation of established theory and techniques in movement, incorporates fresh approaches, and presents the combined material in a logical and systematic manner. The theory was developed during Ms. Sabatine's extensive experience as a teacher of movement and choreography. The resulting text is distinguished by a clarity of thought and a precision of language that makes the work readable and accessible—even to the non–dance-oriented reader.

Ms. Sabatine is an expert at blazing a clear trail. She is well trained in presenting her material in a cogent, step by step, organized fashion. The text provides numerous photographs to aid in comprehension of the exercises and theory. Appendixes aid in selecting music to match the tempo of the exercises and provide a course syllabus along with suggestions for planning individual classes.

While *The Actor's Image* will be an excellent sourcebook for teachers and students of movement, its appeal will go beyond that segment of the artistic world. I can envision the book's becoming a trusty reference for directors, acting teachers, and drama students. For example, directors might use one exploration or series of explorations outlined in this book to suit their own specific cast situations. Acting teachers will have a new friend in Ms. Sabatine's clearly stated theories and techniques.

I have no doubt that Ms. Sabatine's book will be warmly welcomed. It is a generous and thoughtful gift she has given us—a work that will be hungrily consumed by academic and nonacademic theatre/movement professionals everywhere. *The Actor's Image: Movement Training for Stage and Screen* will nourish, satisfy, and delight its readers for years to come.

David Young
American College Theatre Festival

PREFACE

For the movement specialist and nonspecialist alike, this book provides a guide to a developmental approach of teaching movement for actors. For actors and directors the book provides as well many tools that can be used in the development of characterization either independently or collaboratively. To all theatre specialists it provides a concise theory and philosophy that produce a practical and conceptual basis for analyzing what we see—and to help us all to see better.

Especially important is the chapter on exercises, which provides the reader with a complete physical warm-up, complete with illustrations necessary to understand each one, descriptions of what each is designed to do, how each one relates to the whole warm-up process, and cautionary notes on how to know when an exercise is helpful or harmful to your body. One of the appendixes contains a list of music selections that will help in the enjoyment of the exercise, and that also provides a framework for judging the optimum tempo of each exercise.

One chapter deals solely with a step-by-step process of exploration of various techniques for body awareness and concepts of movement that leads the reader to an understanding of the relationship of mind and body. The value of each exploration is enhanced by its relative placement, and explanations of the lessons to be learned from each exploration as well as the detailed discussion of the elements involved.

Finally, the applications chapter gives the reader a technique for using the explorations in a systematic approach to characterization. Although the worth of this work can be determined only by its practice, interested parties have an opportunity to observe how it is accomplished—by supplementary photographs of actual applications, and a supportive chapter by a practicing professional concerning his use of the theory in three separate characterizations, in three distinct theatrical styles.

ACKNOWLEDGMENTS

I would like to acknowledge the contributions of David Hodge and David Samuelson, for without their encouragement this book might not now exist.

CREDITS

All photographs processed by Curt G. Matthew.

Photographs in the applications chapter are by David Hodge.

Photographs in the exercises chapter are by James L. Horvath.

Line drawings in the exercises chapter are by Nan Cadorin.

The subject in figures 3-1 through 3-127 is James Sheerin.

The subjects in figures 5-1 through 5-12 [Animal Essence Exploration and Intention Essence Exploration] are Gary Chase (light top, dark pants) and James Sheerin (dark top, light pants).

The subjects in figures 5-13 through 5-27 [Animal Essence Exploration and Emotional Essence Exploration] are Geoffrey Dawe (dark top, dark pants) and Robert Phillips (light top, light pants).

1
INTRODUCTION

Part of the purpose of this book is to impress on the theatre audience at large the value and intricate nature of the area we loosely call "stage movement."

More important, however, included in the body of material are many techniques and concepts useful to a wide body of theatre artists and valuable to anyone confronted with the problems of bringing a text alive—or for that matter of creating a text. In many instances the title of director could easily be substituted for the terms "instructor" or "teacher." And, while I am specifically referring to "movement teacher," an "acting teacher" can just as easily use (and many have used) many of the techniques I describe.

I employ this device partly in the interest of maintaining a consistent focus and partly because I feel the need to express the concepts within a *movement* framework. Although actors, directors, and acting teachers may not then be directly addressed, it is not because their interests or needs are not encouraged or met, but that there is a far greater need and interest I mean to arouse.

Ideally an actor should be thoroughly trained to deal effectively with the three areas essential to performance on the stage: acting, voice, movement. Because of the practical improbability of finding a towering talent capable of mastering and teaching all three demanding disciplines, the current philosophy in theatre today is to find specialists in each discipline and to weld them into a single effective team to provide a coherent unit, providing effective instruction to developing talent in their separate and mutually supportive areas.

This is a wise and seemingly inescapable philosophy and one to which most theatre artists willingly subscribe. Each of the three disciplines incorporates a wide body of material within it and requires the utmost care and many years of intense training and experience to produce a capable teacher. Common sense dictates the employment of three highly trained specialists (who are intelligently aware of the requirements and basic application of the other areas involved) to effectively deal with the task of training competent professionals.

Practically speaking, however, many teaching situations fall short of this ideal, and in those cases certain ad hoc adjustments can be made to approach a workable version of the conservatory ideal. A single theatre generalist or a specialist in one of the three primary areas may be asked to fulfill one or more of the specific areas outside his or her area of specialization. When this happens, the only recourse is to fall back on the literature available pertaining to those areas he or she may not feel totally secure with. Although there are many lucid, well-written texts to aid one in the acting and voice areas, there are none to equal them in the movement arena.

This text is designed in part to fill that void. It deals effectively with the practical problems of conditioning the mind and body of student actors, using a broad base of tried and proved movement techniques. It is not a survey of various specialized approaches but a coherent, cohesive, and practical body of material that is focused and directed by easily comprehended theory.

This text, in part, is also designed to fill another void. To date there has been no generally accepted model of a course in basic movement for actors. Granted the fact that there are many exceptional movement specialists in theatre today, there is still no generally accepted text dealing with the fundamental goals or the techniques, theory, or philosophy necessary to achieve those goals for training actors in basic movement. This text is designed to provide the first (and, we hope, not the last) words specifically aimed at effectively dealing with this problem.

If, at least, agreement can be made among a majority of specialists concerning the essentials of a basic course in movement for actors, perhaps a more lucid body of literature may begin to evolve concerning the relevance, relationship, and application of some of the many relevant movement specialties. When should a student study movement and dance of certain periods and styles? Are gymnastics, weightlifting, or circus skills important to an actor's development? How can Aikido, Karate, or T'ai Chi be helpful or harmful to an actor? How much should

3

or need an actor know? How do we best approach the further physical development of an actor?

We cannot even begin to ask those questions until we, as a body of specialists, agree on the desired nature of the basic course in movement for actors. This text provides the essential framework of such a course, combined with a healthy body of material necessary to give it substance and coherence.

Before we begin to discuss movement for actors' training, we must address several questions. The first is: What disciplines are *not* movement for actors' training?

Mime, ballet, modern dance, jazz dance, T'ai Chi, karate, physical education, rolfing, fencing, stage combat, Alexander technique, acting, effort/shape, and the like—none of these disciplines is movement for actors' training in and of themselves. However, almost all the pioneers and teachers of movement for actors' training have begun as students of one or several of these disciplines because there were no training programs for movement for actors. What they had to do was find elements of their training that they could adapt to the task. This is what every teacher must do. It is certainly beneficial for a teacher of movement for actors' to be exposed to as many of these disciplines as possible. But to think that any one of them in its pure form would be training for movement for actors would be a gross error and a disservice to the student.

In short, only Movement for Actors' Training *is* movement for actors' training.

Eight years ago I was awarded a grant from the Pennsylvania State University to investigate the various approaches to the subject of movement for actors. I interviewed some of the leading pioneers in the field at the time, and discovered that almost every person interviewed had begun teaching one of the aforementioned disciplines as movement for actors only to realize that more was needed.

For instance, Joseph Gifford, a movement teacher of many years who had been a student of Charles Weidman, Doris Humphrey, and José Limon, said, "I taught what I knew, dance technique; thank God, after the first year I turned around and looked at what I was doing and realized it was absolutely the wrong thing. I was tying them in knots. They weren't going to be dancers."

Sophia Delza, author of *T'ai Chi Chuan* (New York: David McKay, 1961) pointed out that T'ai Chi has nothing to do with any performing art. One does T'ai Chi for one's self; it is a ritual art that can be experienced only by the performer.

Robert Moulton, a former student of Louis Horst, Martha Graham, and José Limon who took his early inspiration from Laban noted, "At that time [late 1950s and early 1960s] it was thought by many in the theatre that if an actor was really feeling inside all the edges were supposed to take care of themselves. You would speak right and move right." He discovered that that really didn't happen, so he knew the

4

purely internal focus was not enough, but he also discovered that though the Graham technique worked well for *Oedipus Rex* it didn't work for contemporary drama. So he, as the others, had to modify his concepts and approach to movement training for the actor.

Aileen Crow started as an actress, and progressively studied dance, effort-shape, and Alexander technique. Although she has taught classes in each of these disciplines, her movement theory and practice consists of a blend of all three. If any of them had been sufficient to her needs, she would not have had to create an amalgamation of them in order to teach movement for the actor.

Louis Campbell has studied many disciplines including Lecoq mime, and although he believes in that discipline as a learning base, he readily admits that mime has its own private gestural language alone that cannot fully cope with "intention" or "character." It is, as he points out, an excellent discipline for "precise articulation of physical form" and offers a superb process for freeing an individual. However, he is highly eclectic by nature, and thus bonds the many separate philosophies and disciplines he has studied to his area of physical interest. But of course, any of these disciplines may form a firm *foundation* for the future teacher of Movement for the Actor.

Finally, Robert Benedetti, who is not really a movement specialist at all, but rather a director, writer, and teacher, has authored at least one important book in the field. In his book, *The Actor at Work* (Englewood Cliffs, N.J.: Prentice-Hall, 1970) the base of his concept for total acting training is the belief that such training can come about only in an atmosphere that supplies study in voice and movement as well as in acting. I agree with Benedetti's philosophy; therefore, the best environment for this training is in a conservatory approach in which the acting, speech, and movement teachers function as a unit with a group of actors so that they are working as a team of skilled and knowledgeable specialists who understand each other's task and orchestrate their individual efforts toward the common goal.

Once one agrees with this hypothesis, it should become evident that if a movement teacher is unfamiliar with the other disciplines and unable to alter his or her technique to fit in with the common goal, then he or she is unprepared to teach movement for the actor. The movement teacher must be familiar with the disciplines of voice and acting in order to design their training program to achieve maximum effectiveness.

That is the key to this discussion: The design is ultimately more important than the approach. As I have demonstrated, each of these experts in movement came from a different orientation, and found that the discipline in its pure form was not movement for actors' training. Each had to adapt their primary discipline (or disciplines) to change its orientation and the philosophy behind it in order to deal adequately with the task at hand.

There are any number of possible foundations to build on, but the ultimate end form must inevitably reflect the same concern—which is not to produce a Modern dancer, or ballet dancer, or mime, or even a gymnast—but to help to train an actor. And this requires a concern for more than just physically conditioning the actor.

The discussion thus far leads us to a second question: What *is* Movement for Actors' Training? It is simply a program of classes designed to provide an actor with awareness and control of his physical, mental, and emotional instruments. Moreover, it should be designed so that the actor has techniques available to deal with his or her own alignment, tension, breathing, and movement and acting problems once his or her trainer is no longer there. In short, Movement for Actors' training is a program of instruction that guides talented, intelligent, and sensitive individuals to become versatile experts in their own stage movement. Ultimately, then, the goal of the actor's movement training should be the integration of mind and body; the whole organism must be in harmony with itself so that it is ready for interaction.

Important lessons that the actor must learn are

proper alignment

proper balance of tension and relaxation

proper breathing techniques

proper warm-up techniques

an understanding of his or her own body

the ability to neutralize his or her personal mannerisms

understanding of basic movement elements (space, time, energy, and so on)

understanding of mind/body connection (so that movements are motivated)

the ability to work with others

the ability to work alone

independence from constant monitoring

the ability to apply acting technique to movement problems

the ability to apply movement technique to acting problems

the art of centering

proper use of internal and external techniques

The *basic* requirements to become a specialist in Movement for Actors' Training are as follows:

sound acting training

thorough understanding of the body and body mechanics through anatomy and kinesiology courses experience in verbal and nonverbal improvisation (exploration) techniques

sound dance/movement training

experience teaching acting and movement courses

working under the direction of a movement specialist

understanding of voice

All other specialized techniques or disciplines are supplementary and of secondary importance.

I have taught in this field for more than twelve years, and I can say with certainty that study in all the aforementioned areas are not by themselves enough to produce a teacher of movement for actors. It is necessary for the teacher of movement for actors to specify his or her own theory or philosophy of movement. He or she needs to set a goal for his or her movement for actors' training. (What do I want my students to acquire from this?)

Finally, each teacher must develop a system that he or she will use to guide an actors' growth in understanding and ability. Of course, all teachers in any field must have a clear and understandable reason, objective, and system to guide both student and teacher—but so few people understand that movement training also requires discipline, order, and method. (I have found it necessary to state this fact all too often.) A teacher of movement for actors needs to have a plan of action, which is the main goal of this manuscript: to provide a plan of action for a *basic* course in movement for actors.

This book is the product of eleven years of research and practical experience with actors and directors in various professional training programs based on a conservatory approach to actor training. The theory has evolved through lessons learned from the students and their teachers in classes designed to teach movement for the stage compatible with and complementary to simultaneously taught and coordinated acting and voice classes, that is, a conservatory approach.

Generally speaking, the acting theory I used as a working model for the development of my approach to movement training is known as the Method.* The Method is more dependent on the inner realities of the actor and the character than on the purely external manipulations of the voice and body. This external approach I refer to as "technique."†

*The Method is a realistic style of acting in which the actor strives for close personal identification with his role.

†**Technique** (tek nēk'), *n.* **1.** the method of procedure (with reference to practical or formal details), or way of using basic skills, in rendering an artistic work or carrying out a scientific or mechanical operation. **2.** the degree of expertness in following this. *(a pianist with good technique but poor expression)* [my emphasis].

[From: *Webster's New World Dictionary of the American Language,* Second College Edition, William Collins and New World Publishing Company, Inc., Cleveland and New York, copyright 1972 and 1970].

I believe that both methods, or approaches, are valid. Indeed, no actor functions without his own particular blend of both "technique" and the Method. Therefore, any movement training for the actor must appeal to both areas of the student's mentality in order to give each individual the opportunity to find this balance within himself.

It was with this belief that I initially approached the task of creating a coherent and practical method of movement training for the actor. I have now worked in theatre and dance for many years and retain that belief. My training and experience have led me to the inescapable conclusion that the mind and body are a single entity. Although this statement is, in itself, neither new nor novel, I am constantly surprised by the number of people in theatre and dance who overlook, ignore, and even scoff at this notion.

The evidence of a profound connection between the mind and body is overwhelming. Unless an individual willfully prohibits it, the body invariably reflects the emotions and intentions of the mind. When the body is tired, ill, strong, or weak, the mind responds accordingly.

The interaction of mind and body is universal. This is not to say that the connection between the two is an invariable constant whereby we can eliminate all consideration of individuality. On the contrary, the interaction of mind and body, although universally present in mankind, is as different from person to person as are the potentialities of both.

Not every person will react in exactly the same manner to a given situation. When cornered, one man will cower in fear, another will turn in anger and fight, and still another will merely stand dumbfounded. I do not propose that understanding even crudely the connection between the mind and body can help us to predict any individual's reaction to a given situation, nor is prediction a desirable or important consideration at this point. I do propose, however, that whatever the individual's reaction is mentally it will manifest itself physically.

This is the single most important concept used in the formulation of my theory of stage movement. It is central to all the material contained in this book, and the guide by which I teach. From this single unifying concept comes all the other guiding principles of my work.

One of these principles is individual development and choice. Because each of us as individuals possesses a unique set of strengths and weaknesses, I find it important to frequently stress to my students that each person will progress at a rate different from his fellows. He will find exercises that will speak more profoundly to him than others and he must choose to use what works for him and not worry whether someone else is getting further ahead or dropping behind. Some will have excellent strength and endurance but poor coordination; others have patience and elasticity but low energy and drive.

The most important message here is that training or performing is not a competition. Unless a healthier attitude is encouraged, students tend to compare themselves (and actors are no exception to the rule). This competitive attitude may well be appropriate and desirable for track and field, but it is unsuitable and even destructive to the pursuit of self-awareness and self-development.

Therefore, I stress that it is not success that is important (that is, a good-looking or flashy product) but personal commitment to developing self-awareness, understanding, and compassion. It is important that each person realize that he or she is on his or her own quest, and that the exercises and explorations I provide are not tests but opportunities. Each student must understand that although there will be things he cannot do and others that he can easily accomplish, exercises or entire lessons that he will seemingly gain nothing from, and others that he will soar with—none of these potential occurrences is related to victory or defeat. They are the very essence of self-discovery—the first step toward development as an artist.

It is an ideal toward which we are working, not a product. This is a process of self-discovery directed toward finding a more complete grasp of the connection between mind and body. This mind–body connection is the key to organic acting, where the inner realities of the characer are revealed through the *actions* of the actor. The goal is always ahead of the actor. He should be trying to make maximum use of his body, intellect, experience, and sensitivity in creating and performing a character for the purpose of communicating an idea the playwright-director wishes to illuminate.

The actor must develop a certain discipline that will allow him the proper blend of control and freedom to help in the achievement of the ideal.

Many experienced actors are concerned with this ideal, and many of them have dedicated themselves so thoroughly that they have evolved their own method of achieving that ideal. These fortunate few have found what works for them and continue to seek for it when it is necessary, when the challenge is great enough, and they must be admired for it. George C. Scott supposedly never had an acting or a movement class in his life, and yet his characters consistently have a vibrant, believable, and understandable life. But what of the less fortunate, less experienced majority who have not found the necessary formula? A single startling exception to the rule does not mean that all actors should abandon training entirely. On the contrary, a majority of professional actors repeatedly come back to the classroom in a continuing effort to perfect their craft.

Beginning, as well as advanced actors, must be aided toward the continuing development of their own discipline. The system of movement training I have developed is not the panacea—it is not *the* special formula that guarantees success in producing great actors. The individual is responsible for creating his own methods. But I have developed a consistent, coherent philosophy that has guided me (and that can guide student and teacher alike) in organizing the intellectual and kinetic growth and development of the actor. Ultimately this method can give the actor the discipline and tools with which to function in his craft.

My method is a system of movement *exercises, explorations,* and practical *applications* (of exercises, explorations, and theory) designed to awaken the student to certain truths about himself and his relationship to the world in order to maximize his potential as an actor. Ultimately it is the actor who must find the blend of internal and external methods that he will use in his work. The student must find for himself the balance of mind and body. The actor is responsible for his choices. He must determine how he best functions, and find the keys that operate the many mechanisms within him which only he can know.

The teacher must provide an atmosphere of trust, cooperation, direction, and focus to the class. He or she must, of course, be sensitive and responsive to the needs of his or her students and balance discipline with creative flexibility in order to allow maximum growth.

In the following program, I have developed a series of exercises to be performed daily as part of a mind–body warmup combined with explorations of the body, and other basic elements of stage movement (that is, space, time, energy, gesture, music, intentions, action-verbs, and so forth) designed and ordered in such a way as to reveal possibilities and limitations for each student. Because each class of students is unique, alternate exercises and explorations have been suggested as well as the creative additions of individual instructors and the intelligent adjustment of class routine and order of topics covered.

Although I have placed the exercises and explorations in the order I try to follow in my classroom, I vary this orderly progression when it becomes necessary, and sometimes find this to be extremely beneficial for the class.

However, I would advise reserving the "Abstractions" or "Essence Theory" concept until the indicated time period. It is an extremely difficult concept to communicate or assimilate, and if the student hasn't been prepared by the necessary physical and mental conditioning, "Essence Theory" could prove to be useless (and even a great frustration) to him.

It is a complex and misunderstood field we are dealing with, and one that is extremely young in its development. Future teachers will refine the work present experts have begun, so it is important that they receive as much support and the best and most thorough information on training techniques and theories that have been discovered to date.

Special Note: Because it is so little understood, and because I believe it deserves special comment, I would like to restate my belief that movement training for the actor is a separate discipline from any other.

I am an expert in both dance and stage movement, and while both my dance and stage movement classes benefit from my expertise in both, they are separate disciplines and must always be treated as distinct entities. This is why I can so ardently proclaim that training in mime, stage combat, or T'ai Chi is *not* movement training for the actor.

They are all excellent and fascinating supplementary disciplines—as are ballet, modern dance, and Alexander technique. A student of acting or a stage movement teacher can only benefit from supplementary training in these areas—but a person trained solely in any of these supplementary areas is neither a teacher of movement training for actors nor has he or she as an actor had adequate training in movement for the actor.

Also, although I have studied and taught extensively in dance and movement of various periods and styles, this is another entirely separate discipline which, although it may be extremely beneficial to the actor in his craft, fails to deal with too many realities of the actor and his task. My task in these classes benefits from students trained with my movement theory because the actors will understand that the movement of the period was natural and appropriate (that is, organic) to those people because of their dress, lifestyle, and social expectations. But an actor specifically and solely trained in this discipline will be sadly lacking in the many other tasks he or she will face in the modern theatre—even if he or she only expects to do Shakespeare in the park for the rest of his or her life.

2
THE PROGRAM

- *The Organic Nature of Acting*
- *Assumptions*
- *The Three Stages of Training*
- *Movement Training is Collaboration with Acting Training*

The program I have designed is a system of movement training that assures a solid, broad starting point, maintains a developmental progression, and extends the actor's abilities in such a way that he can confidently expect to be effective in a host of acting styles. Where appropriate I have drawn on certain of the special approaches to movement (giving credit to those approaches or their originators where possible and appropriate), but have sought to maintain the sense of a firm central technique, a nucleus of skills from which ventures out into peripheral studies can be launched without the risk of losing one's place. This central technique is guided by my philosophy of movement training, discussed in the introductory chapter, and which I will return to periodically throughout this text. Because this is such an important concept, I shall restate it here.

THE ORGANIC NATURE OF ACTING

Briefly, I believe in the organic nature in the craft of acting. Simply, this means that the actor's only tools of expression are his voice and body

guided by his mental and emotional attributes. The
tween the actor's physical, mental, and emotional
organic entity. Therefore, any training must seek t
organic entity. In this nuclear design, then, the acto
allowed to grow in a controlled way. His awareness of,
his technique and his organic development shoul
Finally, his range of acting and movement accomplis
suit.

There are certain assumptions to this program for movement study.

Movement Specialist

First, the instructor must be someone trained in both acting and dance,
a movement specialist. Any training lacking this combination—such as
an acting coach in a crash workshop in modern dance, a dance
instructor invited in and handed some acting texts, or a fitness expert
cautioned, "no, not calisthenics exactly ..."—is likely to bring about
some painful experiences for all concerned. No matter how much dance,
mime, fencing, or gymnastics one might have mastered, there is no
substitute for direct and deep training in acting *and* dance.

Supply the Foundation

Second, this program assumes that the goal for acting is an ability in all
kinds of theatre styles: naturalistic, period, romantic, children's, nonverbal, from comedy of manners to Theatre of Cruelty. This program is
designed to establish a foundation. It cannot promise complete polish in
any style, but the actor will be ready to pursue specific areas of study
that directly relate to any specific theatrical mode in which he is
interested or compelled toward.

The Conservatory Situation

Third, this program was devised in a conservatory-type teaching situation, wherein the stage movement study is integrated with the work of
the acting and voice coach, frequently resulting in a series of in-class
projects and productions that are the product of a three-way collaboration. Stage movement study has its well-marked dimensions, and the
study works best when the students are pursuing separate but related
voice and acting training.

t, the basic course seems to fit about a one-year course of study (see ample course syllabus in Appendix 1.

THREE STAGES OF TRAINING

On these assumptions rests a three-stage developmental progression: *exercises*, *explorations*, and *applications*.

Exercises

The initial phase, the exercises, is devoted to the fundamental tasks of conditioning the actor's body, making it strong, sensitive, and supple. Like any educational process, this work involves adding and subtracting: adding endurance, suppleness, awareness, economy and precision in moving, and related qualities, while simultaneously stripping physical quirks and customary bad movement habits, including awkward gesture, excess tension, a casual carriage, and most basic, an inexpressive immobility. In effect, the task of the movement specialist is to try to restore the actor's body to the natural grace and ease it was intended for at birth, before the body developed all the tics, slouches, slumps, and masks that social experience imposes on bone, tissue, and the emotions. The goal is a finely tuned instrument capable of expression and articulation of fine nuances clearly and effectively.

Explorations

The second and more advanced explorations unit takes the actor further along the path toward his renovation. As he continues to condition himself through a daily discipline of a growing number and variety of exercises, he will be led to explore his inner nature and his relationship to the world around him—including other people. Through a series of studies on space, time, energy, gesture, and emotion, the actor learns what he does as he walks through space, how he orients himself to the world by time, discovering what he and most peole do *kinetically* relating to other people and their world. In the explorations unit, the actor learns everything he can about how his body can be expressive, and how the world looks when seen in terms of movement. He will begin to understand how his internal reality effects his movement. He will be able to see how physical environment effects his internal reality. Through experimentation he will learn that by adjusting his physical mechanism he can effect his inner being and, conversely, that through

16

simply applications of the Method (sense-memory, emotional recall, and so forth) he can effect the way his body moves. This is the most exciting and valuable point in the development of an actor in stage movement training. At this point the actor begins to understand his organic nature. This organic nature is simply the connection between his mind and body. The actor's inner knowledge of how the mind and body mutually effect each other is the key to his further development, and the ultimate goal of this section of study. Then, with his knowledge, he can begin to concentrate on applying his learning by adjusting his inner and outer realities in order to effect a different persona; that is, characterization.

Applications

In the applications unit I have tried to arrange a sequence of movement studies that will bring the actor to the doorstep of characterization. The actor must continue to acquire a range of movement experiences so that he has a large movement vocabulary to employ in the various kinds of applications he will be asked to provide in specific acting assignments. I try to achieve this by giving assignments of an increasingly specific nature based on the student's accumulated expertise as it applies to characterization. For instance, in the early stages of this section, I will ask students to find (through observation or intuition) the walk of a character they are familiar with or are working on, and much later I will ask them to find and express through movement and major intentions of their characters in a given scene. The intent of this portion of study is to focus the student's mind and body on the problem of applying his growing awareness and skills to some specific project. From the broad base of experimentation and exploration, he then moves into the more specific area of application.

MOVEMENT TRAINING IS COLLABORATION WITH ACTING TRAINING

It is in the applications that the expertise of the movement specialist may seem to run afoul of an acting coach or a director who feels characterization falls solely into his province. Movement is primarily toning up the body, fencing, and the like—harmless (but useless) space analysis in the acting coach's view. This is a political issue in the profession, and there is no sense in proposing a pat way to deal with what can be a thorny situation. But let me emphasize that just because I attempt to deal specifically with characterization does not mean that I believe movement classes alone can effectively eliminate the need for sound acting training. Nothing can! Rather, this attempt reflects my belief that we should use every tool available to assist the actor in the development of his total mechanism. My goal in approaching characterization through movement is to provide another possible avenue of growth as a collaborative and supportive effort designed to aid the acting coach. The point is not to engage in polemics. Rather, it is to perceive the full spectrum of movement training, from subtracting physical deficits all the way up to the physicalization of a stage character.

3
EXERCISES

- *Relaxation: The First Step*
- *Posture and Alignment: The Second Step*
- *Breathing: The Foundation*
- *Spine Studies*
- *Centering: Finding the Source of All Movement*
- *Isolation Exercises*
- *General Exercises*
- *Floor Exercises*
- *Ending the Warmup*
- *Comments and Suggestions*

Suppose for a moment that you are an actor who desires to master the physical mechanism. How do you approach this project? The key is the desire. All else follows from that key element. If you want to fully develop your own body, you must first envision its full potential, which is invariably a great deal more than you may first imagine. You must aim toward an ideal version of yourself. Otherwise, all your early aches, strains, and awkwardness will lead you to believe that your old, familiar physical shell is intractable, hopeless stuff. Yet, you must discover your own limitations, and the unique gifts and liabilities you must work with. One body may be loose and limber, thus adept at stretches; another may be tightly strung, giving it a compactness and a surer balance. Unless you (as each actor must) clearly understand that your body is unique, you may be led into a false security or despair simply by looking around and comparing apparent progress. Thus, your work may become ineffective. You should think realistically, remain mindful of unalterable pecularities in your physical make-up, and strive to become aware of all you can do to attain your ideal.

  The movement instructor can be particularly helpful in this

regard. In some cases the instructor may have to devise special exercises for individual students to work on in or outside of class to overcome certain blocks and to keep them in pace with the rest of the class. Later, exercises may be devised and adapted to specific acting projects. Most useful to the student initially, however, is a reliable set of fundamental exercises and some basic principles.

This chapter contains a set of exercises I have found effective, which are organized by a few basic principles I believe essential for movement training for the actor. The key idea to keep in mind in developing your own exercise regimen—both in teaching it and in performing it—is to follow the proper developmental sequence. Basic principles must come before elaborate or complex movements and concepts; slow, easy work must come before the fast and arduous. Most important of all, *do not* try stretches in the early part of a day's work. Many dancers and fitness buffs go right onto the floor, first thing, and tug viciously at their muscles to get themselves stretched out. Not only is this hazardous, but it is also stupid since the opposite result most frequently occurs. Preventing injury while stretching and strengthening the body depends on executing a proper sequence of exercises. So, for example, pliés should precede jumping and stretches. The other important aspects of this work are to continually encourage proper breath and energy flows, the economical use of force, and the proper blend of tension and relaxation.

I have exercises that deal with these concepts specifically, but because of their universal nature, the student's attention should be focused on them repeatedly—especially breathing. Proper breathing helps counteract excessive tension, and encourages proper energy flow, which allows for more economical application of force. On the other hand, improper breathing technique (such as holding the breath or shallow chest breathing) promotes needless tension that inhibits energy flow and prevents economical application of force. In other words, above all else, I continually remind my students to breathe.

The technique offered here is but a sample of the kind of basic and sequential work needed, and any instructor will need and wish to supply many more exercises. With assistance, the actor will find those exercises that are most helpful for his specific problems. The basic objectives of this stage of training are to eliminate needless tension, achieve a functional balance between tension and relaxation, condition the body for strength, flexibility, and endurance, and develop awareness of the body, that is, a kinesthetic sense. These objectives should provide the principles for selecting all further exercises.

Most of the following exercises can be done to music. I find that music aids both my control of the exercises (by freeing me from setting and maintaining a tempo, thus allowing me to aid the students' efforts), and gives the student a certain guide by which to move. I have found that rock and commercial jazz are best to use because they provide a heavy bass beat. For each exercise that can be done to music I have suggested more than one piece of music (see Table of Tempos, Appendix 3) for an idea of what I consider to be an appropriate tempo once the students have learned the movements. In teaching any exercise, of course, it is best to work at a very slow easy tempo without music. The instructor may use a hand drum or simply call out the counts and movements.

RELAXATION: THE FIRST STEP

The first step in the developmental process is to reawaken an awareness of the body's natural, relaxed condition. This is a difficult first step since tension is our society's boogeyman.

Tension is a neurological phenomenon that combines mental strain and taut muscles. Most tension is unnecessary. Anxiety is an incompetent way of coping with most feared eventualities, and overly tense muscles are useless even in physical emergencies. (Stanislavsky's often cited proof of the inefficiency of tension involved his asking an actor to perform mental acts while under the strain of hefting a piano.)

Excess tension cripples our emotional, mental, and physical well-being, but all movement, acts, and thoughts proceed from some amount of tension. The trick is to recover the capacity for relaxation while retaining the right amount of tension. This is the body's natural, relaxed condition.

To help the actor to an awareness of this state, the first step should be to provide the experience of utter and complete relaxation. Then the actor is ready to progress to the next level of kinesthetic awareness. In the following exercises this level of complete relaxation should be attained as a prelude to any exertions, and returned to periodically between short periods during which the attention is focused on movement in order to further reinforce the sensation of total relaxation. In both exercises the movement teacher should also try to bring a sense of calm to the students' minds so that this feeling of well-being aids the relaxation process. The instructor's voice can be artfully directed to modulate the audile atmosphere with slow rhythms and a soft tone. Soft music and soft lighting also help.

ATTENTION FLOW

1. Lie flat on the floor with face up and eyes closed. Place the arms, slightly bent, along the sides and allow them to fall into a comfortable position. Extend the legs straight out along the floor away from your head and allow them to roll outward in a comfortable position.

2. Release all the joints in your body. Breathe gently in and out, in and out.

3. Feel your body sag into itself. Feel the gravity. It is a heavy, distinct force, but it is not oppressive.

Once the actor assumes this position the instructor guides him into an utterly relaxed state by moving his attention over his entire body, part by part, successively directing his awareness from one extremity to its opposite. Like a gentle wave or tide, the instructor's voice sweeps the actor's attention across his body, briefly pausing over minute portions of the body, in a regular and calming advance. At each brief pause the actor becomes specifically conscious of a muscle that he then loosens and drains of its tension. For example:

4. Feel the muscle of your right calf. Feel how it rests lightly on the floor, where it touches the floor, how the floor forces the top part of the muscle to bulge up and out. Feel the tension in your calf dissolve and drain slowly into the floor.

5. Now move your attention up your leg, through your stomach, your chest, neck, face, to your forehead. Feel the tension in the muscles there. Release those muscles. Imagine your forehead broadening and opening. Let the eyebrows fall naturally into place and the scalp collapse. Feel the tension lift from your forehead as your entire head begins to float freely in space.

Special focus should be placed on the centers of tension: forehead, neck, and shoulders, most commonly. Ideally, once the actor passes his attention through his body in this manner, he will discover how many parts of his body he never notices, and now feels them absolutely limp. In practice it may require some concerted effort to break down a student's resistance to relaxing. Panic in the face of this process of collapse is uncommon, but it is not a strange anxiety, and its effects may resemble the proverbial description of what it feels like to die a slow, easeful death. (One also thinks of Socrates narrating the progress of the hemlock in his body.) But anxiety should dissipate as the student begins to savor the lively sensations of relaxation and the awareness of how much of his body he can actually feel. Most students greatly enjoy the exercise. It is helpful to frequently return the student's attention to his breathing, to fix his mind only upon his breathing. The routine should be done every day for several weeks, in much the same way every time, so that the student can gain the ability to talk himself into this condition when alone. Mastering self-induced relaxation is the first step to mastering tension, but it is not an easy or quick process.

Complete relaxation collapses the body into a sort of rag doll. Complete tension hardens the body to stone. To move at all and to move economically we must strike a balance. To reach the proper balance we must start with the limp body, so we can slowly escalate the degrees of tension we generate for precise tasks and movements, and closely observe and remember the degrees of tension we are employing for each task. This is all the principle of economy of movement entails, and its chief function is to avoid using too much tension to perform a muscular task.

TENSE AND RELAX

Begin this exercise lying on the floor in a completely relaxed position. Then, one at a time, tense individual muscles and observe how each one is working. Then make combinations of tensed muscles; building up to a totally tensed body. Finally, return to a complete collapse. This process should be a dramatic one, and if the effects are not obvious enough or sufficiently gradual, repeat the exercise.

TENSE AND RELAX SEQUENTIALLY

This exercise is conducted exactly as the previous exercise, except that the tension/relaxation process is executed sequentially from the toes through the legs, buttocks, stomach, fingers, hands, arms, chest, neck, and head. Especially important in this version is that once a body part has been fully tensed and relaxed, no tension should be allowed to creep back into it—especially while the focus is on another body part.

1. Begin the process in the toes on one side of the body. Tense and relax only the toes on that side, then include the foot, then add the calf, then the thigh. When the entire leg is tensed, it should be lifted slightly (no more than one inch) from the floor. When it is relaxed the leg should fall suddenly to the floor as all the tension rushes out of it. Feel the warm tingling sensation—the complete weightlessness of the entire leg free from all tension. Feel the relief of complete relaxation of just this leg.

2. Repeat this entire process on the other side of your body—remembering to maintain the relaxation in the other leg—move the tension/relaxation process through your toes, then the foot, the calf, and your entire leg. Once again feel the sensations of complete relaxation now in both legs.

3. Tense just the buttocks and hold the tension while you insure

24

that the legs are still relaxed—then relax your buttocks. You should be free from all tension from just below your waist down.

4. Continue with the stomach and then move to the fingers on one side of your body. Proceed with the tension/relaxation hand, forearm, then full arm, raising it off the floor slightly. Then, collapse it back to the floor. Repeat the process on the other arm.

5. Now just the chest muscles—no stomach—no shoulder tension—then just the shoulders. Lift them off the floor, then on to your ears and back down. Now let them collapse. Take some time to feel the relaxation below your neck. Pass your attention through every part. You should feel as though you are floating slightly off the floor.

6. Proceed with this process to the neck, then to the facial mask. Work your face in many different ways. Open your mouth and eyes wide, and raise your eyebrows—then move all the muscles in the other direction so that the eyes squint, teeth clamp, and lips stretch wide. (Be careful that tension is only in the face.) Now work your facial mask every way you can. Then relax. Concentrate on your breathing.

7. Finally, tense every muscle in your body and hold it several seconds while you tighten; tighten each muscle—now collapse. Let all tension drain out of you into the floor. Feel it drain away as you fill yourself with warm fresh air as you breathe in and out, in and out.

MINIMUM EFFORT MOVEMENT

1. Extend your arms and legs out to their natural limits and slowly return them to your sides, carefully employing the minimum amount of muscular tension needed.

2. Next, move from this supine position to a seated position.

3. Then move to a standing position through the same process.

Throughout these and similar routines involving elementary movements, the actor will be surprised by how little tension is actually required to move his body about. He should also be pleased with his resisting the temptation to apply a sudden surge of tension to execute a simple movement. Such simple movements are self-instructive, and it is only by the actor's observing and making kinetic notes inwardly that the lessons of tension and relaxation can take hold. Once he has a firm sense of controlling tension in simple moves he should progress to more

25

complicated and arduous feats. His pleasure should grow as he finds he almost never needs a great amount of tension, even in apparently arduous tasks. This should promote confidence and, in the long run, inspire creativity.

The relaxation and tension work is most essential in the early part of the training when the actor is still not all that familiar with his body. I find it useful, however, to return to this work from time to time, especially when the actors are experiencing stress and tension during, say, a difficult and challenging assignment. If at a later stage in his training, a student becomes nervous or frustrated about an Exploration, and thus tense, this is the ideal time to return to relaxation work. Once again, the technique for discovering the minimum amount of tension needed is directed toward the actor's being able to work on himself, at will, and knowing when it is necesary to employ, such as in classic instances of stage fright. In the Applications unit I will discuss a theory of characterization based on gradations of tension (see Chapter 5).

POSTURE AND ALIGNMENT: THE SECOND STEP

The term *posture* is frequently misread to imply a frozen, inert stance, a carriage somehow stilted and formal, as opposed to natural standing and walking.

This is unfortunate, especially the confusion between what is "natural" and what is habit. Perhaps the point is too obvious, but it cannot be overstated. What typically happens to our body in growing up is that we acquire distorted and misshapen ways of holding ourselves.

We slouch, sink, slump, shuffle, laze awkwardly and inefficiently upon our frame, generally undermining the very purposes of our skeletal structure. Unless our attention is forcefully called to what is slovenly in our posture or carriage, we remain blissfully ignorant of our distortions. Often, too, one grows fond of his favorite distortions, thinking this little slump is "really me," and it requires some tact to point out otherwise. Frequently it is these distortions of posture and alignment that thwart clean, expressive, and efficient movement.

For an actor, such problems spell professional disaster; he drags his misshapen image into every characterization, and unless his bad habits happen to be extraordinarily captivating, leading into a career as a popular single-type character actor, his professional opportunities to drag himself into characterizations are likely to be severely limited. One caveat, and it is the opposite danger: The actor who has so perfected his posture, alignment, and carriage that he has become enchanted with his new self, and drags it beautifully into every characterization, making all roles resemble one off-duty ballet dancer. Stage movement works to recover the lost potential for the natural development, an ideal posture and a free carriage. So the goal is to learn one's ideal posture, at least to know it well enough to leave one's more glaring idiosyncrasies behind in the wings, and with this mastery, to recreate any other posture in a characterization he pleases. So let us start with the immobile body and readjust the frame, which all our muscles—the agents of movements— have shaped.

The logical point at which to begin, then, is in the simple, natural erect stance. Metaphorically, the body consists of layers of blocks that must be stacked directly on one another, in a state of equipoise, over one's center of gravity. If one block is out of line the whole stack is distorted, balance weakens, movement grows awkward. For example, slouched shoulders cause the pelvis to tilt, which in turn thrusts the buttocks out. The tiers of a body so arranged are precariously stacked and are ill fit to move well. Walking in such a posture produces a heavy amble and places undue stress on the heels.

There are several alignment problems that occur fairly frequently. Some of these are problems quite apart from the usual "cool slump" many teenagers and younger adults endeavor to effect. These are, in many cases, irreparable problems caused by the original construction of the spinal column in the individual, because of accident, illness, or habitual and continual poor posture. In each case involving a problem with the spine, great care must be taken not to try to force it to do anything that may cause further problems. In every instance the person involved will either know beforehand, or must be encouraged to seek medical assistance to discover the cause of any great discomfort involved in any exercise. Ruptured or herniated disc, scoliosis (lateral curvature of the spine), fused spine or fused vertebra, and foreshortened spine are but a few of the many problems that may be present or that may even be misrepresented or misunderstood by the sufferer. These are serious problems that only qualified medical specialists can deal with. Fortunately, pain is a fairly accurate measure and should be heeded in all cases.

Most problems, however, are not so severe. Most common among these are: the placement of weight either too far forward or back (Figure 3–1); the shoulders and head slung forward (Figure 3–2) or back (Figure 3–3); the shoulders tensed up toward the ears (more common with men, see Figure 3–4); the pelvic tilt (more common with women, see Figure 3–5); or some combination of these problems. In order to solve these problems, the major goal for both actors and teachers is to correct one's self-image (the internal personal image of what is good posture) and corresponding kinetic feeling of proper posture.

FIGURE 3-1   FIGURE 3-2   FIGURE 3-3

28   FIGURE 3-4   FIGURE 3-5

Natural Alignment*

Let us straighten out this crumbling structure and start from the foundation.

1. First get the feet parallel (or just slightly turned out if exact parallel is too difficult to manage) about six to eight inches apart. The weight of the body should plummet straight down, directly to the center of the space between the feet, a little in front of the ankles.

2. The knees should be released, not locked back, or bent.

3. Lengthen the abdominal muscles by pulling across and up, as if you were trying to flatten your stomach. (The stomach muscles are designed to hold your internal organs in position. By pulling up vertically and laterally with your stomach muscles, you simultaneously lose the unnecessary bulge, align your spine, and place your internal organs in their proper position.) This will put the pelvis directly in line with the center of the body rather than tipped back.

Natural Alignment

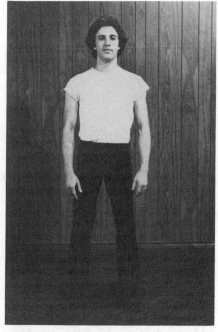

FIGURE 3-6   FIGURE 3-7

*See Figures 3–6 and 3–7 for frontal and side views of good (that is, natural) alignment. See Figures 3–1 through 3–5 for examples of poor alignment.

4. The rib cage must be in a neutral position (that is, not tilted forward, back, left or right) and the chest lifted (as though there were a string attached to the exact center of your sternum and someone pulled evenly and gently at a 60 degree angle toward the ceiling), which in turn will broaden and lengthen the back.

5. Shoulders are dropped and relaxed, neither pressed forward nor pulled back.

6. The back should be left open by not pinching the shoulders together.

7. The head is lifted and balanced squarely on top of the spine, and the neck is relaxed.

Now we have each level of the body properly stacked and aligned, with the center strongly built for all subsequent moving. At first it may seem peculiar to try on this alignment, but it is your natural alignment, and the balance, poise, and readiness it confers on you will soon seem very natural.

Alignment Tests 1 and 2

FIGURE 3-8   FIGURE 3-9

The correctly aligned position (that is, natural alignment) must be tested. Here is a sample test:

1. From what you feel is the natural standing position, start with the head and slowly curve the spine down until the hands touch the floor; the feet remain flat, and as you move into the final collapsed position, the back is smoothly curved, the legs are slightly bent, and the hands are grazing the floor (see Figures 3–11, 3–10, 3–9, and 3–8 in that order).
2. To resume the standing posture, straighten the knees and slowly reassemble a lengthened back by successively straightening the spine to an erect line (see Figures 3–8 through 3–11).

If in the collapse and ascent, you can hold your balance, the posture passes this test as "natural." If not, start over.

FIGURE 3-10   FIGURE 3-11   FIGURE 3-12

Alignment Test 2

This is the best method I know for determining whether you are aligned properly. It may be added to the end of Alignment Test 1 or it may be done independently. I use it at vital transition points during the Exercises and Explorations.

1. From a natural standing position press up through your feet onto your toes. (By press up, I mean to apply a steady even flow of energy so that you rise up slowly, rather than pop up quickly [see Figure 3–12]).
2. Then come back down slowly through your feet until you are again in your natural standing position.

If you had to shift your weight forward or back to press up onto your toes, your alignment is off. If you had to shift your weight forward to rise, you probably stand with your weight too far back on your heels (and you are not prepared to move). If you had to shift your weight back, you are probably either bent forward at the waist, or you're leaning too far forward with your weight too much on your toes (and you have little capability for any but forward movement).

There are other tests one can apply, but the main stress is on the actor's learning to don his proper alignment at will until it becomes second nature to him.

BREATHING: THE FOUNDATION

Breathing is the foundation of our organic nature. The breath brings to us life-sustaining oxygen and carries away the poisons of our bodies. Breathing provides fuel for the mind and body. A secondary function of breathing is to provide the vocal cords with the means for operation. Fortunately, the same rules that govern the efficient production of vocal expression also govern the efficient production of all other muscular efforts. These rules include the proper blend of tension and relaxation, proper alignment, and harmonizing breath patterns with patterns of movement.

This does not mean that I wish to eliminate the need for the speech or voice teacher. On the contrary, my work in breath control is designed to assist in the establishment of positive habit patterns in this collaborative process of actor training in an area where our responsibilities happily overlap.

I say happily because one cannot overestimate the benefit of good breath control for the actor. And the more positive reinforcement a student has, the more likely he will quickly establish good habits and proper control through consistent attention on correct technique.

Going back to beginnings, the guiding principle involved in my methodology is the development of the student as an organic entity. This first involves developing his organic awareness of himself. Each step so far has led him in this direction, but breathing provides the best key and most obvious example of the organic connection between mind and body.

Breathing is largely an autonomic function which the novice actor takes for granted, but it can also be consciously controlled. In approaching the breathing mechanism, then, we are subtly exploring the rudiments, or more accurately, the basics of the organic connections of the mind and body.

Once again the ideal is to harmonize breath patterns with movement patterns. Only such a harmony will enable a moving actor to speak (and move) well, or permit the speaking actor to move freely. Of course this is obvious. But it is equally obvious that many actors have not mastered this technique, because there are so many panting and puffing actors struggling through performance after performance for apparently little or no reason.

In some exercises approached for the first time it is beneficial to focus the student's attention on the principles before beginning. Breathing is one area in which it is *not* beneficial to forewarn the student that he will be focusing his attention on this aspect of himself because a self-conscious conceptualizing behavior will interfere with his autonomic function. So in the first approach to breathing it is wise to use a misdirection technique so that the student will find himself observing his unconscious breathing and then move slowly into control unself-consciously. Any number of misdirection ploys will do. Here's one that is very effective.

WALK, RUN, WALK, LIE DOWN

1. Walk in a leisurely manner around the room. Just relax and enjoy yourself.
2. Now pick up the pace as though you had somewhere to go. Walk faster and faster. Observe how this affects you.
3. Now you're in a hurry. Take it into a jog; then into a run. Take your time at each level to feel what this does to you.
4. Run as fast as you safely can. Notice how this affects you.
5. Slow quickly back to a walk.
6. Slow the walk until you stop.
7. Now gently lie down on your back and get your breath back. Notice how you feel. Close your eyes.
8. Feel the difference of this position. Feel the air rushing in and out of your body.

9. Relax. Continue to get your breath.

10. Relax down into the floor, as if it were a big feather bed. Feel how comfortable this is. You should be breathing naturally now, easily, slowly. In and out. In and out.

11. Feel how pleasant it is to just relax. Just breathing slowly, naturally in and out.

12. Move your attention, keeping your eyes closed, just allowing your mind to focus on your breathing. Feel how your diaphragm expands as you breathe in and how your chest lifts slightly at the very end of the breath. Breathe in and out. In and out.

13. Feel how your chest and diaphragm collapse gently and easily as you breathe out.

14. This is your natural breath rhythm. This is how you were meant to breathe.

15. Try not to change or control your breath pattern as you observe the mechanics of how you breathe naturally. (This will force the students to apply will power and control their breathing—which is part of the lesson. Although they won't know it, they are now on the threshold between subconscious and conscious control, which is the point I have been working toward. The attempt not to engage in conscious control while consciously observing the phenomenon is a vital and intricate organic movement.)

16. Although it is difficult not to effect your breath pattern as you focus on it, try to relax.

17. Try to continue breathing naturally, keeping your breath pattern even, smooth, and uninterrupted as you rise to a standing position. Find the easiest, most economical way to get to your feet, and once you've started, don't stop, so that you don't interrupt your breath pattern.

18. Now once you're up, try to feel the same relaxed sensation of how you were breathing on the floor, with your diaphragm expanding and collapsing as the air comes in and out, in and out.

19. Now find your alignment.

20. Open your eyes, press up through your feet.

21. And relax. Shake out the tension.

22. Let's talk about it.

When the students get to step 21 in this exercise, and are told to relax and shake out the tension (signaling an end to the exercise), generally there is a huge intake of breath and a long sigh as the class as a whole releases their conscious control of their breathing apparatus. Usually someone from the class will point out that it became very difficult to continue abstaining from conscious control of the breathing once their attention was focused on it, and that controlling the breathing in an effort to keep it natural was even more difficult.

This is natural. When a student is told "focus your attention on your breathing, but don't interfere with it," for the first time, it is like saying "don't think about yawning" or "don't think about alligators." Eventually this will be an easy exercise for the student. It should become almost automatic; that is, the actor should be able to use his ability to find his natural breathing pattern as a means to eliminate tension and provide proper breath support for speaking and movement. This ability should become as effortless for him as finding his balance on a bicycle, and just as with bicycle-riding skill, he will never need to relearn it once he truly has done so.

THE MECHANICS IN MOTION

Let us observe breathing mechanics, and how these relate to movement.

1. First lie on your back on the floor, arms at your sides, and relax.
2. Inhale and note the tension as the filling lungs lift first the diaphragm, and then the chest, outward.
3. Now exhale and feel the relaxing muscles as the torso collapses.
4. Repeat the process several times and exaggerate slightly the tension and relaxation, inhaling more deeply and exhaling more fully.
5. Next, experiment in breathing in a variety of tempos: quick, irregular, at long intervals, and so on.
6. Then try mating tempos with simple movements done in the same tempo. (For instance, lift the arms slowly over the head as you inhale in a matching tempo. Bring the arms down sharply as you exhale in a rush all the air.)
7. Now stand and starting at Step 2 go through each step until you are mating movement with breath. Note the similarities and the differences in the effort needed to achieve the proper breathing technique at each stage of the process between the standing and lying positions.

This second exercise can be repeated intermittently rather than daily. On each return to it, students should move more freely and adventurously as their breath control and muscular coordination and strength improve. This exercise reveals that, to a greater or lesser extent, all

35

exercises are breathing exercises, since one should always seek to mate breathing with movement. So, especially in the early training process, continual reinforcement of proper breathing with movement is essential.

Once again, this kind of experimenting is aimed at learning to phrase inhalation and exhalation rhythms to a sequence of exertions. This is an area of constant concern for me as a movement teacher and I return repeatedly to this thesis while teaching all other exercises because proper breath control is essential to all the actor's endeavors. As you can see, this is an area where the voice and movement specialists must have overlapping responsibility because the actor needs to master breathing more efficiently. Basically, the actor needs to work on deep breathing, opening his lungs to their full capacity. Mere gulps of air, our ordinary skimpy intake, do not permit a sufficient amount of oxygen into our system for a smooth and flowing performance in the strenuous work ahead.

SPINE STUDIES

As a special way to heighten the awareness of the actor's natural posture and the importance of the skeletal frame, especially regarding breathing, let us briefly examine the spine. The spine is a part of the body that most people never think about until they injure it. Actors cannot afford that luxury.

The spine is that linked column of vertebra that keeps us erect and permits us to move. To get the feel of how the spine works, divide it into three separate parts: the upper back (that series of vertebra from the head to just below the shoulder blades), the middle back (that series of vertebra from the shoulder blades to the waist), and the lower back (that series of remaining vertebra from the waist to the coccyx at the base of the spine). Gently experiment with bending. Try to feel how each section bends. Notice that each section slightly overlaps the next (since totally isolated movement of one vertebra is impossible).

It is usually a pleasant surprise to discover that one can actually bend one's middle spine. Just knowing that the poor, neglected, nonsensitive (except when it's scratched, and then it can be ecstatically sensitive) back has a life of its own, with parts to be moved and observed, should prove stimulating for the actor in his labor toward a more expressive body.

Here is an exercise for warming up the spine.

SEQUENTIAL RELAXATION

1. Assume an aligned stance with feet parallel and arms hung naturally at the sides (see Figure 3–7).

2. Drop the head forward and round and relax the upper back. Just relax and hang into the muscles, feeling the weight for eight counts. Then very gently bounce the upper back eight times in the same eight-count tempo. (Let the arms hang naturally throughout this exercise.) At this point the hands should hang about mid-thigh (see Figure 3–11).

3. Now add the middle back and hang for eight counts (see Figure 3–10). Then bounce both sections as one piece for another eight counts. Do not raise the shoulders; keep them relaxed. Hands should hang about knee height.

4. Now add the lower back and repeat the hang and bounce (see Figure 3–9). Do not release the pelvis. The hands should hang about midway between the knees and ankles.

5. Now release the pelvis and allow gravity to pull your body head-first toward the floor directly in front of and between your feet, with your arms hanging naturally, hands touching the floor (see Figure 3–8). Don't bend the knees. Keep the whole spine relaxed. Repeat the hang and bounce.

6. Now slowly and sequentially, stage by stage, bring the body back up to the beginning, erect, naturally aligned stance. Take eight counts to come up. The pelvis rotates forward (as the torso lifts up) and comes under as the lower back rotates up into place, then the middle back comes vertebra by vertebra into place, and finally the upper back comes up sequentially. The head should continue to hang forward, because the neck should be totally relaxed until the last moment when that portion of the upper back slides back into place.

7. Once back to a standing position and aligned and centered, relevé* (that is, press up through the feet onto tiptoes) and test your balance (see Figure 3–12). Slowly come down through the feet. If any shifting of weight was needed to relevé, the center is not precisely located.

8. Repeat the exercise (Steps 1 to 7) again in eight counts at each stage. If prepared, repeat again in four counts per stage.

The next exercise is also for the spine but helps with breath control and alignment as well. Each of the exercises in this spine series should also develop awareness of, and greater flexibility in, the spine.

BREATHING IN

1. Start from the position in Step 4 of the last exercise, but with knees bent (see Figure 3–8). Bend over and relax, then inhale in

---

*Hereafter I will refer to *relevé* simply as relevé, or I may alternate with the direction to "press up through the feet," which I find a helpful image for actors.

eight counts. Exhale for eight. Now, inhaling in eight counts, sequentially bring yourself up: straighten legs, pelvis tucked, lower, middle, upper back in place.

2. Then gradually release your breath, exhaling for eight counts, as you slowly and sequentially return to position at start.

3. If both raising and lowering is fully sequential and the breathing timed with it, move on to repeating the exercise in four counts. Then, when ready, two counts. Caution: Always keep the movement in control and always stay centered.

Now let's try a variation—a slightly more vigorous exercise that is good for the circulation and utilizes a different approach to the spine.

SWING AND UP

1. Start in the same position as in the last exercise, that is, over and relaxed, with knees bent (see Figure 3–13). Gently bounce the head up and down, four times.

2. Swing the head and neck from side to side, right, left, repeat. Be sure the neck stays relaxed. Let the body breathe naturally with the movement.

3. Now add the shoulders, arms, and torso into the swinging,

Swing and Up

FIGURE 3-13   FIGURE 3-14   FIGURE 3-15

right (see Figure 3–14) left (see Figure 3–15), right again, but let the swing carry you up (see Figure 3–16) erect at the peak with the arms reaching toward the ceiling, then let gravity drop you down toward the floor on the left back (see Figure 3–17) through the original position. Repeat in the reverse direction. Repeat on both sides.

4. Then, after the fourth swing, stop applying force and allow gravity to bring the body gradually to a halt. With the body returned to the opening position, slowly come up through the spine, as in the first two exercises, straightening legs, bringing the pelvis under, rotating up through the lower, middle, and upper back to natural alignment.

5. Test your alignment. Relevé up, and come slowly down through the feet.

These exercises for the spine are important for a variety of reasons. Probably the most important reason is that the musculature involved is more specifically and directly related with the breathing mechanisms than with any other body part. The spine provides the primary structural support for the entire upper body, and is assisted in this function by the musculature of the back, chest, and abdomen. It is vital that this musculature be strong and flexible—and that it be warmed up early in the exercise session so that the spine is protected from possible injury.

FIGURE 3-16   FIGURE 3-17

Also, although for the sake of convenience I have titled this section spine studies, it must be pointed out that a more significant principle is actually at work here. It is called the principle of centering.

CENTERING: FINDING THE SOURCE
OF ALL MOVEMENT

The guiding principle in our discussion thus far has been to encourage organic awareness and development. One of the prime tools I use to do this is the concept of centering. Centering is merely the process of finding one's center. This is difficult for most people, only because most people have never thought that they had a "center." For the movement teacher, as well as for the actor, this is an essential concept that is both useful and operative on many levels.

Let us start with the dictionary definitions of the term and then discuss them as they apply to movement.

> **Center,** n. **1.** a point equally distant from all points on the circumference of a circle or surface of a sphere. **2.** the point around which anything revolves; pivot. **3.** a place at which an activity or complex of activities is carried on (a shopping *center*), from which ideas, influences, etc., emanate (Paris, the fashion *center*), or to which many people are attracted (a *center* of interest). **4.** The approximate middle point, place, or part of anything. **5.** A group of nerve cells regulating a particular function (the vasomotor *centers*). —v.t. **1.** to place in, at, or near the center. **2.** to gather to one place; gather to a point. **3.** to furnish with a center.*

It is obvious that none of the above definitions specifically deals with the human body or being, but the concepts provided can be used to aid us in our task as teachers and artists.

Generally then, the torso, from the pelvis to the neck, can be thought of "... as the point around which anything revolves; pivot ...," since the arms, legs, and neck are all attached to it. The spine, the rib cage, and the surrounding musculature can be construed to be "... a place at which an activity or complex of activities is carried on ...," since most of the major organs and bodily functions take place there.

It must be noted that, for a variety of reasons, each individual's center is different from his neighbor's even when they have both attained their ideal postures. Looking at the general case, however, we see that there is a correlation between the center of the torso and the definitions of center as "... a point equally distant from all points on the circumference of a circle or surface of a sphere ... ." A lateral cross section of the chest cavity, viewed from the vertical, reveals an elliptical or oval shape (see illustration on p. 41) whose center is equidistant from the corre-

*Webster's New World Dictionary of the American Language, Second College Edition, William Collins and New World Publishing Company, Inc., Cleveland and New York, copyright 1972 and 1970, p. 230.

sponding sides of the ellipse. Vertical cross sections of the torso when viewed from the lateral reveal two ovals (see illustrations below) whose centers are displaced by volume toward the larger end of the shapes. These three conceptual reference points roughly correspond to a fist-sized spherical shape that is located at the bottom of the sternum in line with the vertical spine and midway between the ribs on either side and also midway between the front and back of the chest cavity.

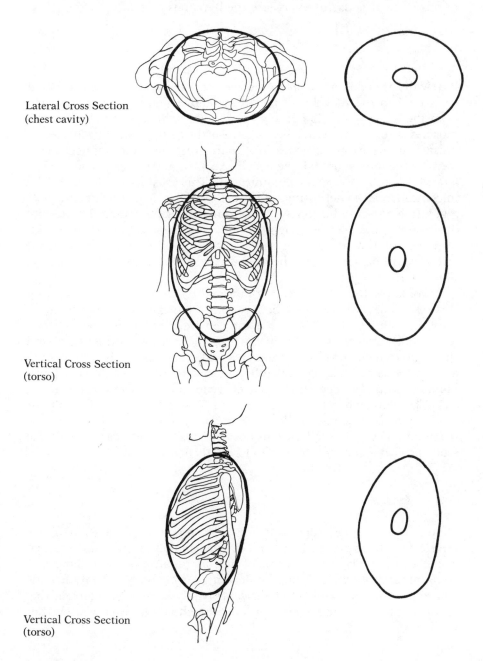

Lateral Cross Section
(chest cavity)

Vertical Cross Section
(torso)

Vertical Cross Section
(torso)

It is no accident that this reference point exists. Man is a bipedal creature and so depends on a symmetrical shape. Also, since he stands erect, with most of his weight in his upper body, he must have a high center of gravity.

Specifically, however, I believe the center is "... a place ... from which ideas, influences, etc., emanate ...," because all movement should have its origin in the torso, that is, the center. This is a difficult concept to prove but it is useful to explore the hypothesis.

The Physical Center

Physically this means that the muscles of any major body part, being connected to the muscles of the torso (and dependent on the oxygen from the lungs which is borne by the blood, which is supplied by the muscles of the heart, which lies in or near the center), must be alerted to initiate the necessary preparations to execute the contemplated movement or the movement will be poorly executed and appear disjointed as a result of the poor organic commitment. This thesis is borne out by the inference from the definitions of the center as "... a group of nerve cells regulating a particular function ...," and also by the awareness that the decision to move does not originate in the muscle itself, but in the brain, from which the impulse is carried, through chemically stimulated electrical impulses, down the spinal cord through the torso to each muscle group involved.

We know that this action is initiated by the brain, and following this reasoning, we are led to believe that the origin of all movement is the brain. But is it not true that the constant interaction of the body (continually receiving and transmitting information to the brain) and the brain (which constantly measures and evaluates the incoming data and responds by sending back different information) form an inseparable and mutually dependent unity of reception and response?

Therefore, when I speak of the center I am referring to that point or area at which the constant flow of impulses gather to one place as they pass on their way to their various destinations, so that I can provide the student with a conceptual tool to focus his further effort.

The Mental Center

Mentally the center, especially for an actor, is an extension of his physical center, since all ideas and designs are fed through the physical center to the body. The actor must do this because he is working in a communicative art form, and he depends on his body to actualize his concepts. A mathematician could conceivably solve a problem in theoretical calculus without needing to so much as raise an eyebrow, but the actor's problems demand that he use his physical instrument almost constantly to solve his problem—or at least to test his solution.

I would also like to point out that the mathematician subliminally alters his physical state while focusing on his problem. This means that the degree and type of mental activity occurring in a human is (regardless of profession or race or sex) ultimately linked through some sort of organic balancing, measuring, and monitoring system that is designed to produce the ideal physical state for that activity. This system is a function of what I call centering.

The Emotional Center

What of the emotions? How do they relate to this concept of the center? First let us examine what we call emotion. The definition of emotion is:

> **emotion,** n. **1. a.** a strong feeling; excitement. **b.** the state or capability of having the feelings aroused to the point of awareness. **2.** any specific feeling; any of various complex reactions with both neutral and physical manifestations, as love, hate, fear, anger, etc.*

It is emotion that provides the key to understanding the concept of center and that unites the seemingly isolated mental and physical aspects of humanity. Any emotion seems to begin as a physical sensation in the area of the torso near the heart and spreads outward to the extremities. Observe athletes in their reactions to winning or losing a contest and you will be able to actually mark the progress of the impetus to scream in pain or leap in joy at sudden changes of fortune, you can see their bodies begin to crumble and sag from the center as the certainty of defeat begins to dawn upon them, or begin to swell outward from the center as they realize the nearness of victory.

Athletes serve so well for this because their focus is so keen on the competition at hand that they become unself-conscious about their emotions. They are spontaneously reacting with their entire being to the events transpiring around them.

Small children are also excellent to study in this regard because they too are uninhibited about showing their emotions. If you observe a child who is dramatically surprised by, say a door slamming, or a sudden bump on the head, you can actually watch as his face changes from normal concentration to total surprise where his eyes and hands fly open and his entire body lifts from the center to an effort to gather enough outside data. Then, while he is still in that position, his attention focuses inward to gather still more information from his body. Then, as

---

Webster's New World Dictionary of the American Language, Second College Edition, William Collins and New World Publishing Company, Inc., Cleveland and New York, copyright 1972 and 1970, p. 458.

he comes to understand the situation, his chest will begin to collapse from the pain or hurt, or inflate with pleasure or joy.

When I speak of the center, I am referring to the area in the midchest where all action originates, where all reaction first manifests itself, the small area of the upper torso we must position in relationship to the rest of the erect body so that it provides the proper balance of forces to effect natural balance, and the conceptual focus for the student's future development of his organic unity.

Center provides a conceptual framework to focus the student's various endeavors in the class. Through the concept of center the student will develop an understanding of himself as an organic unity of mind and body, and not as a series of unrelated parts. Thus by the mere mention of the word "center" in the right contexts, the student will begin to form his own definition of the term that will accomodate the various uses to which I put it. As he forms his definition, he will be unconsciously using his physical sensations, emotional reactions, and intellectual powers. He will, in other words, be forming an organic understanding of the term, while taking his first steps in finding his center—which is the source of all movement.

This process of finding one's center I call centering, and forms the basis for the development of the organic entity.

I have placed this preliminary discussion of the term here in order to provide a link between the first exercises and the others to follow. Since all movement comes from the center and depends on proper breathing techniques, the quality of the movements and their execution are linked not only to the developmental process described earlier (wherein slow easy work precedes complicated or physically demanding exercises), but also to the necessity for total body awareness and commitment to tension-free execution of seemingly isolated movements.

ISOLATION EXERCISES

All parts of the body should be rediscovered for their unique properties of movement: Isolating each part to analyze it independently by moving it is the principle at work here. The neck, for example, is seldom thought of in terms of its movement. Working on moving the neck forward, sideways, and backward, the actor should find an amazing flexibility. With concentration and discipline, he can uncover a similar elasticity in the shoulders, rib cage, and pelvis. These parts are normally somewhat immobile compared to one's hands, arms, and legs, but if an actor can learn to rotate his rib cage, he will rethink the possibilities for motion inherent in his more dynamic body parts. Through repeating carefully controlled isolation exercises, he can discover how supple the human body can and should be. By simply unlocking the muscles he can acquire a sense of fluidity, grace, and precision in his movement.

Isolation is the single most important path to a supple and expressive body.

HEAD ROTATION
FOR RELAXATION OF THE HEAD AND NECK

1. Put the feet in parallel position and properly align the body.
2. Drop the head forward and down; slowly rotate the head to the right, to the back, to the left, and then forward in eight counts. (Allow your jaw to relax and fall open as your head rotates toward the back and close the jaw as it comes forward again. Also, let your head hang naturally as if it were a weight suspended from a short elastic band—don't push it forward, back, or to either side—just apply the force laterally and let the head do the rest naturally.) Keep the flow of energy even.
3. Repeat the same exercise to the left. Once you have mastered the movement in eight counts, do it in four counts.
4. This exercise helps to relax the muscles of the neck. It also helps one to obtain more fluidity by inhaling on the first four counts (as your head moves toward the back) and exhaling on the last four counts (as your head moves toward the front).

HEAD PERCUSSIVE

1. Begin with your feet parallel and your body aligned.
2. Drop the head forward on the first count.
3. On the third count bring the head center to the original position.
4. On the fifth count drop the head back to the limit of the neck's ability to move in that direction until you are looking at the ceiling, but do not throw your chest out or you'll be off center.
5. On the seventh count bring the head back to the center.
6. Repeat steps 2 through 5 taking two counts for each movement.
7. Then, after you have completed the entire (forward, center, back, center) pattern twice, tilt the head to the right side in two counts without changing the angle of your face to the front wall (that is, you should still be looking at yourself in the mirror, with your head tilted to the side) [see Figure 3–22].
8. Bring the head back to center on two counts (see Figure 3–21).
9. Then, on the next two counts, tilt the head to the left (in the same manner as you did to the right).

45

10. Then bring the head center again on the next two counts.

11. Repeat the right–left sequence again using two counts for each movement.

Once the class as a whole has conquered the basic movements, I then ask them to try the entire exercise using one count for each movement. Some classes require several weeks to reach this point; others are ready to try it in one week. When they have mastered it both ways (that is, when they can do the entire exercise organically, without deliberation or hesitation using either two counts or one count for each movement— and without following someone standing in front of them doing it so that they can copy), I move to the next level of complexity by adding an arm pattern to the head movement. Here is one arm pattern I use to go with this exercise. (To teach it I use two counts for each movement.)

12. As you tilt your head forward bring the lower arms up to the shoulders (by simply bending at the elbows) with the palms of the hands facing the body, the fingers pointing toward the ceiling (see Figure 3–18).

13. As you bring your head center raise both arms to a 60 degree angle toward the ceiling, making certain that the shoulders do not rise—keep excess tension from the shoulders—palms face each other, arms are straight (see Figure 3–19.)

14. Now as you drop your head back, bring your arms out and down to form oblique angles from the plane of your body, so that they are parallel to the floor just slightly below shoulder height, arms are straight, palms face up (see Figure 3–20).

15. As the head comes center again bend the elbows and rotate the arms inward so that the palms come to your chest with the arms still parallel to the floor just below the shoulders (see Figure 3–21).

16. Repeat positions 12 through 15 with the arms as you repeat the head pattern (forward, center, back, center).

17. With the arms in the ending position (see position 5 preceding), as you move your head to the right (see position 7 preceding) open your arms until the palms face forward (see Figure 3–22).

18. As you bring your head center bring the arms back to their closed position (palms to chest and arms parallel to the floor).

19. Keep the arms in that position as the head tilts left.

20. Open the arms until the palms face front again as the head comes center.

21. Keep the arms open as the head tilts right.

22. Close the arms as the head comes center.

FIGURE 3-18

FIGURE 3-19

FIGURE 3-20

FIGURE 3-21

FIGURE 3-22

47

23. Keep the arms closed as the head tilts left.

24. Open the arms as the head comes center.

Notice that the arms only open and close (once the forward, center, back, center pattern is completed) when the head comes center, except for the first initial movement to the side. This is a simple pattern to teach, and is simple in theory, but the coordination of the head movement with the arm pattern (especially the side to side movement) is very difficult to master. So student and instructor alike will want to take time with the initial learning stages. Once this has been mastered, however, the student will have passed a barrier in kinesthetic awareness and muscular dexterity. He also will have opened another door to organic movement because he will have been forced to use his mind much more than his muscles to conquer this exercise, and make it a part of him. Moreover, this exercise forces a new level of ability for centering since the entire body is united in this single purpose—the legs support the breathing-balanced torso while the other extremities move simultaneously, or separately as demanded, while the mind monitors and responds to the various stimuli.

It is really far simpler for the student than it sounds, and he may not realize the importance of his accomplishment, but once he learns to coordinate his breathing with these movements, he will have made a significant step forward toward developing himself as an organic entity.

The next exercise is more subtle, and in many ways more difficult for a non-dancer than any we have looked at so far, but it is the next logical step in the organic warmup because it develops flexibility in the torso.

Rib Cage

FIGURE 3-23   FIGURE 3-24   FIGURE 3-25

RIB CAGE EXERCISE
FOR FLEXIBILITY OF THE TORSO

1. Move the rib cage directly to your right side on count number one (see Figure 3–23).

2. Bring the rib cage back to center on count number two (see Figure 3–24).

3. On count number three move the rib cage to the left (see Figure 3–25).

4. And on count number four come back to center.

5. Repeat steps 1 through 4 three times. Try to match your breathing with your movement. As you move to the side inhale, and as you come center exhale. (*Note:* The tendency is to tilt the leading shoulder up, and allow the trailing shoulder to fall. This should not happen when the exercise is performed correctly. Try to keep the shoulders so that they form a straight line parallel to the floor. Another tendency is for tension to creep into the shoulders forcing them up toward the ears. Concentration on breathing and relaxing them should help.)

6. Now begin again at center and move the chest forward on the first count (see Figure 3–26).

7. Center on the second count (see Figure 3–27).

8. Back on count number three (see Figure 3–28).

9. Center on count number four.

10. Repeat steps 6 through 9 three times.

FIGURE 3-26   FIGURE 3-27   FIGURE 3-28

Note: A good image to use for this exercise is to imagine that you have strings attached to your sternum in front, a corresponding vertebra in the back, and a string also attached to a rib on either side at a 60 degree angle toward the ceiling at each of the four points. There is an equal amount of tension on each string, which holds your center. To move toward the right, imagine the person holding the string on your right side pulls up and away from you to the right. To come back to center, imagine he simply releases excess tension on the string. To move front use the same imagery of the person in front pulling up and away from you. To come center imagine again that he simply releases excess tension of the string. And so on left and back. This image will keep you from slumping into the intended direction of travel, and keep the shoulders relaxed and in a horizontal position, because the focus of attention (and the impetus for movement) is below the shoulders at the center of the body.

Also note that it is essential to have the rib cage area relaxed to allow for freedom of movement. If there is tension in the body, it is from the waist down. When you have grasped the above, you are ready for the next step.

11. Move the rib cage directly to the right side, to the front, to the left side, and back (using only one count for each movement). Then go to the left, front, right, and back. Repeat. Remember to keep the hips stationary so that you are not weaving, and movement is happening in the torso area only.

12. Once you have mastered the above, add on the use of an arm pattern. As you take the rib cage to the right, place the left hand on the head and keep your right hand on your waist, then as you move the rib cage to the left, place the right hand on your head, and return your left hand to your waist. Repeat.

13. Now take both arms slightly in front of your shoulders pointed on a 45-degree angle toward the ceiling, and move the torso, and hold on in the pelvic area, as you rotate right and left. When extending the arms toward the ceiling in front of you, be careful not to lift the shoulders.

PELVIS: SUSTAINED CIRCLING

1. Place the feet parallel, with knees bent and arms down at the side of the body (see Figure 3–29).

2. Move the pelvis slowly in a circle to the right (see Figure 3–30), front (see Figure 3–31), left (see Figure 3–32), and back (see Figure 3–33). The movement should be sustained, that is, have an even flow of energy. Now move left, front, right, and back. Repeat to both sides taking eight counts to complete each circle.

Pelvis Circling

FIGURE 3-29

FIGURE 3-30

FIGURE 3-31

FIGURE 3-32

FIGURE 3-33

PERCUSSIVE PELVIC CIRCLING

1. Starting position is the same as position 1 of the last exercise. Rotate the pelvis in a circular but punctuated pattern. Push the hip right on count one, front on count three, left on count five, back on count seven, then left, front, right, and back. The difference is in the way the energy is applied to the movement. Instead of an even flow of energy the movement is sudden and sharp. You hit the position and hold. (Example: Right and hold and front and hold, and so on.)

SHOULDER ROLL

1. Place the feet in parallel position with the body aligned.
2. Lift the shoulders up and down several times to ease out the tension and relax the shoulders.
3. Lift the right shoulder up on count one and drop it forward on count two. Then lift it up on count three and drop it back to its natural placement on count four. Use the same process with the left shoulder, then repeat the series.
4. Now lift both shoulders up and drop them forward, and lift them up and return them back to the neutral position (four times).
5. Lift both shoulders, twist the right forward and the left back (beyond the neutral position, but not straining), then lift and return them to the neutral position. Repeat, this time twisting the left shoulder front and the right shoulder back.

Afterword on More Exercises

The human body is as fragile as it is subtle and supple. That is why I have stressed avoiding strain. It is crucial that early conditioning work be performed at an easy, relaxed pace, slowly building up strength, balance, endurance, and a sensitivity to the body. The practical goal is for the actor to become an alert monitor of his own organic machinery. He should not be tempted into careless, violent, and wrenching exercise. Instead, he must patiently develop a conscious awareness of his body's capacities, gently leading his body forward, not shoving it beyond its present limits. Shoving, wrenching, and native ambition will slow his progress. Remember, since each person's body is different, progress can't be monitored by comparison. Each person will excell at different exercises and will therefore progress in a manner unrelated to those around him. What each person needs to develop is a relaxed, calm, and thoughtful extension of skills rather than a need to succeed quickly.

However integrated and whatever the other exercises supplied by instructor or actor, it will help to keep an eye on the following principles.

1. The whole body should be warmed up. One part may receive special focus, but everything has to be ready to move.

2. The mechanics of every exercise should be taken apart, studied, or explained. Blind imitation eliminates any chance for internal observation or for the actor to take the exercise home with him. (This is a basic tenant of my philosohy and is the starting point for the development of the mind/body awareness. The actor must understand the purpose, and function—and remember the sequence—of each exercise; otherwise, he becomes a kind of parrot or monkey capable only of imitation. Also, this mindless parroting limits the growth of his kinesthetic awareness.)

3. Preparatory work should always precede strenuous work.

4. Any exercise can be varied or modified for the sake of variety or to focus on a special project or problem.

In these principles and the sample program thus far offered, there is a solid basis for all the additional work that may be necessary or desirable.

GENERAL EXERCISES

The previous exercises have served specialized purposes. They were listed in the order given because they follow the principles of a proper warmup, and follow a sound developmental program of progressive acquisition of skills. Also, in general, these exercises are listed in the same order I use in my daily warmup (see Sample Class Structures, Appendix 2). The next logical step is to provide a series of basic exercises for general toning of the total body. To fill this need I offer the following sample exercises.

STRETCH AND SWING
(FOR GENTLE VERTICAL STRETCHING
AND RELAXATION)

1. With feet in parallel position, lift the right arm straight above the head alongside the ear, and stretch the right side of the torso up with it, for two counts (see Figure 3–34).

FIGURE 3-34   FIGURE 3-35   FIGURE 3-36

2. Lower the arm as you come center for two counts.

3. Repeat with left arm and torso; reach and stretch for two counts.

4. Lower the arm and come center for two counts.

5. Repeat sequence right and left.

6. Bring both arms up together, reach and stretch for two counts (see Figure 3–36).

7. Now, with both arms still above the head, begin to swing your arms and torso forward and down as you bend both knees; releasing the pelvis, and allowing your body to swing down and with the arms continuing down and back until you are a semi-squat with the head relaxed and between the knees, with the arms naturally extended behind you (as though you were preparing to dive off the starting block at the beginning of a swimming race). This all happens in two counts (see Figure 3–37).

FIGURE 3-37   FIGURE 3-38

8. Then swing back up into a flatback position (see Figure 3–38) (see note in paragraph below) in two counts, and hold the position as you gently stretch the muscles in the back of your thighs and small of the back—applying force gently by pulsing in an up and down motion with the entire torso, the hands and arms extending beside your ears and parallel to the floor. Pulse for four counts.

Note: In the flatback position the torso is parallel to the floor, forming a 90-degree angle with the legs, which are straight. (This is sometimes called the table-top position, because the back is straight from pelvis to head, and the table legs are straight, and at 90-degree angles to the table-top.) The face points toward the floor to relieve tension in the neck and shoulder area, so that the neck is in line with the rest of the spine. Especially important is that the small of the back not be rounded (if that is possible, because not all people can achieve this, and it should not be forced). Maximum stretch is achieved the closer you can come to the ideal of a "flat back," forming a 90-degree angle with the legs. Be gentle with this position.

9. Swing down as you did in step 7 above, for two counts.

10. Swing up all the way to a standing position with both arms above the head as you did in step 6. (Use your arms' momentum to help swing you up, in two counts).

11. Lower both arms, using two counts until you are back at the original position.

12. Repeat the entire exercise.

Comment: When you have learned to do the exercise as it is described above, try doing it without bringing your arms back to neutral every time after you've stretched. Just leave out steps 2, 4, and 11. Once you've raised an arm and stretched it keep it aloft (see Figure 3–35). Relax it a bit also, as you raise and stretch the other. This way, the exercise will flow more smoothly.

STRETCH TO THE SIDE, FLAT BACK (FOR LATERAL STRETCHING)

1. Begin in the naturally aligned position.

2. On count one, start to tilt the torso, to the right, while extending the right arm to the side and keeping the head straight front but allowing it to tilt toward the right. Reach toward the wall to your right as if you were trying to touch it. Use two counts to stretch out the torso in this direction. (The stretch should be felt along the left side of the torso, hip, and leg.) [See Figure 3–39].

3. Then use two counts to return to center.

4. Repeat to the left (stretch will be felt along the right side) for two counts (see Figure 3–40).

5. Use two counts to return to center.

6. Repeat right and left.

7. Move into flat back position using four counts to reach the final position with arms extended to the side, slightly in front of the body and parallel to the floor—head in line with the spine, face and eyes looking at the floor. Then gently pulse in this position (to stretch muscles in the lower back and the backs of the thighs) (see Figure 3–41).

8. Slowly round the back and allow the head and arms to relax downward and hang naturally for four counts (make sure shoulders, neck, and back are relaxed, knees are straight). Bounce for four counts.

Stretch to Side, Flat Back

FIGURE 3-39

FIGURE 3-41

FIGURE 3-40

9. Sequentially rise into the naturally aligned position, and relevé to test your balance.

10. Repeat the entire exercise.

Note: Once you have learned the exercise, merely eliminate steps 3 and 5 so that there is a better flow of movement and breath.

Plié Sequence (for Balance, and for Strength and Control in the Legs)

The term *plié* derives from the French word "plier" meaning to bend. When used in its original context the plié refers to a movement in which the feet and legs begin in one of the six classical positions (with the feet and legs turned out to their limit from the hip sockets) and the knees slowly bent so that the knees and feet form the same angle with respect to the floor (see following description of *Classical Pliés*) while the back is held straight and centered. When used in regard to modern dance or jazz dance, the same general principles apply, except that the feet and legs are parallel to each other.

How does the concept apply in a movement for actor's warmup? The plié in the classical (turned-out) positions works to strengthen muscles in the *outside* of the thigh. In parallel position the plié works to strengthen the muscles on the *inside* of the thighs. To exercise the leg muscles fully (as part of a full body warmup) then, both the turned-out and parallel positions should be used.

PARALLEL PLIÉS OR KNEE BENDS

1. Put feet in parallel position, eight inches to ten inches apart, with weight centered.

2. Bend the knees directly over the feet (so that the knees are on the same angle with the feet, which are straight front) in a smooth motion until the heels of the feet are forced to rise. Stop the downward motion just before the heels rise from the floor. This is called demi-plié or small plié. Use two counts for this movement. Bring the hands up to six inches from the shoulders, palms facing the shoulders (upper arms remain in position) as you plié (see Figure 3–42).

3. Rise back to the original position by simply straightening the knees using another two counts (steps 2 and 3 comprise the demi-plié). At the same time raise the arms at a 60-degree angle to the ceiling, palms facing each other (see Figure 3–43).

4. Relevé through both feet on two counts as you open the arms to the side so that you form right angles with both arms relative

Parallel Pliés

FIGURE 3-42   FIGURE 3-43   FIGURE 3-44

FIGURE 3-45   FIGURE 3-46   59

to your body and parallel to the floor, palms facing the ceiling (see Figure 3–44).

5. Bring the palms to the chest (arms still parallel to the floor) as you lower your heels to the floor in two counts (see Figure 3–45). (Steps 2 through 5 comprise the demi-plié sequence.)

6. Repeat the demi-plié sequence making certain the knees go directly over the feet; think of sitting straight down; do not lift the heels or release the pelvis so that your torso tilts forward or buttocks jut out. Keep your back erect, and your buttocks under you.

7. Now comes the grand-plié or full plié. Once again, bend the knees in the same manner as before, except that this time instead of stopping just *before* the heels come off the floor, continue the downward movement, by bending the knees, and allow the heels to rise off the floor, using four counts from the start to finish of the movement (see Figure 3–46). (The arms repeat the same movements this time following the longer counts to go with the larger movements of the legs.)

8. Come back up to the original position by straightening the knees, forcing the heels down as soon in the rise as the mechanics of your legs will allow (that is, don't straighten the knees all the way and then drop down onto your heels). Use another four counts for this.

9. Repeat the grand-plié sequence making sure you don't break the line of the torso forward or backward, or release the pelvis. The lowest point in the downward momentum should occur just before the calf muscles touch the back of the thigh.

Note: The arm pattern should be added only after the mechanics and sequence is understood thoroughly. Also note that this arm pattern is designedly similar to the arm pattern used in percussive head movements, discussed earlier in this chapter.

CLASSICAL PLIÉ SEQUENCE

Once you have learned the entire exercise, proceed with the following sequence of exercises.

1. First position (two demi-pliés, two counts for each movement).

2. First position (two grand-pliés, four counts for each movement).

3. Transition to second (in eight counts).

4. Second position (two demi-pliés, two counts for each movement).

5. Second position (two grand-pliés, four counts for each movement).
6. Transition to first position (in eight counts).
7. Repeat 1 through 6 with transition on other leg.
8. Add relevé to sequence.

CLASSICAL PLIÉS

1. *First position demi-plié* (see Figure 3–48 for demi-plié with arm pattern; see note at bottom of p. 64 for arm pattern).
   a. Start with feet in first position, heels together, feet turned out forming a right angle; and weight centered (see Figure 3–47).

Classical Pliés

FIGURE 3-47

FIGURE 3-48

FIGURE 3-49

FIGURE 3-50

b. Take two counts to bend the knees (it is important to force the knees wide open), knees directly over the feet. As in parallel demi-plié, go down to the point just before the heels are forced off the floor.

c. Then use two counts to straighten the legs to the original position. (Remember, you are now working the muscles on the outside of the thighs).

d. Repeat the demi-plié making certain the knees go out directly over the feet.

2. *First position grand-plié* (see Figures 3–51 [frontal] and 3–52 [side] for grand-plié with arm pattern; see note at bottom of p. 64).

a. Start position after the second demi-plié (when you have returned to the starting position).

b. Once again, bend the knees in the same manner as before, except that this time continue your downward motion through the point where the heels are lifted off the floor, stopping the downward motion before you feel your control of balance slipping, before your thighs touch your calf muscles. (This will be at a slightly different height for each person.) Use four counts for this.

c. Now rise smoothly back to the starting position by reversing the

Classical Pliés

FIGURE 3-51   FIGURE 3-52

process, putting the heels down as quickly as possible; complete the rise by straightening the knees.

    d.   Repeat the grand-plié (steps b and c above) making certain the back remains erect and does not tilt forward or back, and that the pelvis does not release backward or forward.

3.   *Transition to second position*

    a.   You are now back in the starting position.

    b.   Shift the weight onto the left leg and extend the right toe along the floor and directly to the side of the body (making certain both legs stay straight) to the limit of the right leg's ability to keep the toe on the floor with the weight on the left leg. Use four counts for this movement.

    c.   Shift the weight so that the weight is now equally balanced between the two feet. Use four counts for this movement. The heels should be six inches to eight inches apart with the weight centered between them—feet and legs are turned out.

4.   *Second position demi-plié* (see Figure 3–53 for demi-plié with arm pattern)

    a.   You are now in second position (see step c in transition above).

    b.   Bend the knees as you did in first position demi-plié for two counts.

FIGURE 3-53   FIGURE 3-54

c. Straighten the knees as you did in first position demi-plié using two counts.

d. Repeat.

Note: Since the heels *never* leave the floor in second position plié—in neither demi *or* grand should the heels lift from the floor—the second position demi is an estimation of half the distance from standing second and grand-plié in second.

5. *Second position grand-plié* (see Figure 3–54 for second grand with arm pattern)

a. You are now back in second position.

b. Bend the knees again as you did for grand-plié in first—go through the demi position and continue down as far as you can *before* the heels lift from the floor, or you throw your alignment off. Use four counts.

c. Straighten the legs, lifting yourself back to standing second, using four counts.

d. Repeat.

6. *Transition to first position*

a. You are in second position.

b. Shift your weight onto your left leg, allowing your right heel to lift from the floor—keeping your right toe on the floor—using four counts.

c. Bring the right foot back to first position and shift the weight on to both feet, using four counts.

7. Repeat steps 1 through 6, except the transitions shift weight onto the right leg and the left leg extends along the floor.

8. Adding relevé after each plié further strengthens the legs. Merely, rise up on the toes in two counts from the demi-plié position, and four counts from the grand-plié position, and come down in the same number of counts.

Note: There are various arm patterns that can be added once the basics of this exercise are conquered, and as with the arm pattern in parallel pliés, it will aid in coordination and control as well as upper body strength. One such pattern is to raise the arms in front of the body in plié (see Figure 3–48), 60 degrees over the head as you straighten (see Figure 3–49), to the side as you relevé (see Figure 3–49), and back to your sides as you come back to starting position (see Figure 3–50). This will also aid in keeping the hands out of the way of the action of the legs and add a measure of grace to the movement.

SIDE STRETCHES
(FOR THE TORSO AND HAMSTRINGS)

1. Stand in a moderate stride position, feet parallel, twelve inches apart. This is an eight-count exercise. On the first count, move arms out to the side, weight centered. Two, reach left arm up and over the head, and stretch entire torso to the right. Keep the legs straight, and *still* keep the weight centered. Stretch for the remaining six counts, in a very gentle bouncing movement toward the floor on the right. Be sure you are not jamming the muscles (by trying to use maximum force in the stretch and bounce). You are elongating the muscles, not jerking them. Keep the stretch continuous.

2. Repeat on the left side, reaching right arm over the head to the left.

3. Then do in four counts.

LEG EXTENSIONS (FOR STRENGTH,
COORDINATION, AND BALANCE)

1. Feet in parallel position, arms at your sides and out to the side in airplane pose (use a barre, if available, at first). Bring the right leg up to a turned-in passé, foot pointed—two counts (see Figures 3–55 and 3–56).

2. Extend the lower leg (until the entire leg is straightened and extended away from the body along the same line as was the thigh in passé) and flex the foot to the front—two counts (see Figure 3–57).

3. Bring the leg back to passé—two counts.

4. Bring the leg down—two counts.

5. Repeat with the other leg.

6. Turn the feet out, into first position. Move the right leg into a turned-out passé—two counts (see Figure 3–58).

7. Extend the leg out to the side and flex the foot. Make sure the leg is slightly in front of the side position—two counts (see Figure 3–59).

8. Bring leg back to a passé—two counts.

9. Place the leg down—two counts.

10. Repeat to the left side.

11. Feet parallel, lift the right leg up to a turned-in passé—two counts.

12. Extend the right leg directly to the back, with the foot flexed, and make sure the leg stays turned in (see Figure 3–60).

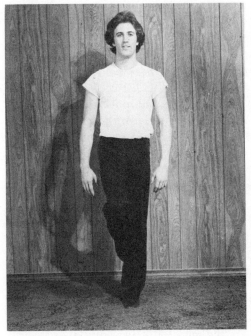

FIGURE 3-55

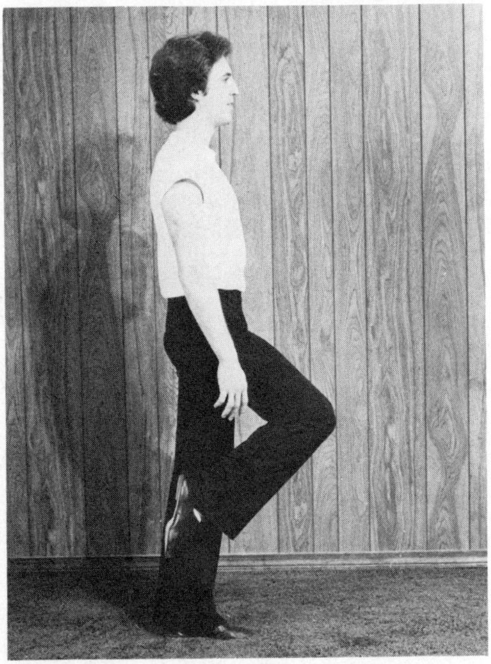

FIGURE 3-56

FIGURE 3-57

FIGURE 3-58

FIGURE 3-59

FIGURE 3-60

FIGURE 3-61

67

13. Bring the leg back to a turned-in passé with the foot pointed.

14. Place the leg down.

15. Repeat to the left.

Comment: Make sure the weight is shifted to the supporting leg in all three patterns, and that you are pulled up through the supporting side (so that you don't slump or lean to that side to counterbalance your weight). The torso should remain directly over the hips throughout.

Variations of the exercise include adding the plié: As you extend the leg, you plié the supporting leg, and as you bring the leg back to passé, straighten supporting leg; or with relevé: After the leg is extended, relevé through the supporting leg (see Figure 3–61).

This and the next exercise are adapted from Matt Mattox (noted jazz dance teacher, actor, and dancer) exercises.

BRUSHES (TENDU) (FOR STRETCHING LEGS, BALANCE, AND COORDINATION)

Tendu is another term borrowed from ballet, but since its specific definition is inadequate to my purpose, it is used here as a reference point or orientation for the informed reader or student. Generally the movements implied or described by this term are correct in that they provide some principles on which this exercise is based. As in ballet's tendu weight is shifted onto the supporting leg while the other leg is extended with the toes brushing along the floor, while the alignment remains centered over the supported leg. But here the feet are parallel (rather than turned out as in ballet), the direction the foot travels is straight front (rather than on the diagonal as in ballet), and the focus is on the toe leading (rather than the heel as in ballet).This form of tendu promotes more naturalistic movement patterns for today's theatre.

1. Feet in parallel position, eight inches to ten inches apart, arms at the side. Brush the right foot forward extending the right foot and ankle completely, while keeping the toe in contact with the floor (see Figure 3–62). Bring the foot back, keeping contact with floor and not bending knee or bending at the hips. Hips remain square to the front. Repeat three more times on the right; then four times on the left foot.

2. Repeat the exercise, again four times on each side, but this time allow the foot to continue forward until the toe leaves the floor six inches to eight inches, lifting the leg slightly, keeping both supporting and lifting legs straight, knees not locked (see Figure 3–63).

3. Lift the right leg, hip height [or higher, but avoid buckling in the torso (see Figure 3–65)], four counts up and four down. Repeat three more times on right, then four times on the left (see Figure 3–64).

4. Reverse the process, working from 3 back to 1. (*Note:* Brushes should be done slowly at first using four counts to raise and lower the leg. Later this timing can be reduced to two counts and finally to one count.)

Brushes

FIGURE 3-62

FIGURE 3-63

FIGURE 3-64

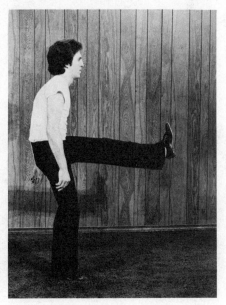

FIGURE 3-65   Wrong

69

FOUR-COUNT STRETCH

This exercise is meant eventually to be performed percussively in a rapid tempo.

1. Place the feet in parallel position, arms down. Lift arms up toward the ceiling, alongside the ears but keep the shoulders down. Weight is centered (on four counts). (See Figure 3–66).

2. Now move into a flat back position, arms in the same relationship with the body, but pointed now at the forward wall, head aligned with spine (on four counts). (See Figure 3–67).

3. Take the body down to the floor and let the palms of the hands touch the floor (if you can't—don't force it) on four counts (see Figure 3–68).

4. Bring body straight up, arms back at the side. Keep weight centered. Do not snap back up in a whip-like movement, but bring the torso and head up as a unit.

5. Repeat steps 1 through 4 again. Keep the legs straight throughout.

6. Now repeat steps 1 through 4 four times, using one count for each movement.

Four-Count Stretch

FIGURE 3-66   FIGURE 3-67   FIGURE 3-68

STRETCH SIDE, FLAT, SIDE, BACK
(FOR LATERAL AND BACK STRETCH)

1. Start in same position as you ended four-count stretch (see the preceding exercise).

2. Lift the left arm up over the head as you lean your body toward the right, and reach toward the right side with both hands in eight counts. Leave the face facing front.

3. Move into the flatback position with arms out in the airplane-wings position. Bounce gently for eight counts. Breathe.

4. Now lift your body up and tilt to the left with right arm over the head and both arms reaching to the left side of the body. Reach for eight counts.

5. Now bring your body erect, bend your knees, bring your arms down to both sides of your body and keeping your back straight, tilt your head back to its limit, look at the ceiling, and bounce for eight counts. Continue to breathe. Let the mouth fall open to keep tension out of jaw and neck.

6. Repeat entire exercise using four counts for each movement.

7. Repeat entire exercise using two counts for each movement.

8. Repeat again using two counts for each movement.

9. Repeat now using one count for each movement.

10. Repeat again using one count for each movement.

LAYOUTS (FOR BALANCE,
STRENGTH, AND COORDINATION)

The layout is a very advanced exercise which, especially in the early learning periods, demand some support for the student. The student should hold onto a chair back, another student's arm, or a ballet barre (if available). After the student can perform the exercise using proper breathing (that is, without holding his breath, or grunting), he should be permitted to try it without support.

1. Feet parallel and arms out to the side. Bring the right leg into a parallel or turned-in passé with the foot pointed toward the floor—two counts (see Figure 3–69).

2. Extend the leg directly forward and flex the foot toward the ceiling—two counts (see Figure 3–70).

3. Take the leg around to the side, directly to the side, not back—two counts (see Figure 3–72).

4. Bend directly forward from the hips into a flat back position, keeping leg directly to the side—two counts (see Figure 3–72).

5. Reverse step 4 by coming up to a standing position leg out to

FIGURE 3-69

FIGURE 3-70

FIGURE 3-71

FIGURE 3-72

73

side, foot flexed and pointed toward the ceiling (you have to rotate the hip under you toward this neutral position)—two counts.

6. Bring the right leg into a turned-out passé—two counts.

7. Bring the knee around in front of you, and place the foot down parallel and even with the other—two counts.

8. Repeat to the other side. Throughout the exercise, be sure the supporting leg is pulled out and not bent.

FLOOR EXERCISES

UP OVER THE BACK, SHOULDER STAND PRESS (FOR RELAXING THE SPINE)

1. Lie on your back, arms at the side, small of back as close as you can comfortably come to being flat on floor, legs together in parallel position.

Up Over the Back

FIGURE 3-73

FIGURE 3-74

FIGURE 3-75

2. Lift legs, then hips and extend legs straight toward the ceiling, toes pointed, with elbows on the floor, put hands under the hips and hold for a moment (see Figure 3–73) before allowing the feet and legs to continue their arc over the head to touch the toes on the floor above the head with the legs straight (see Figure 3–74). Then bend the knees and bring them to the ears (see Figure 3–75). Hang in this position and breathe deeply.

3. Then straighten your legs extending the toes along the floor and lift the legs over your head and hips, and hold once again in the vertical position, with the hands under the hips. Allow your breath to flow in and out. Do not hold your breath.

4. Slowly bring the body down through the spine, making sure to get each part of spine on the floor (see Figure 3–76), and lower the legs (see Figure 3–77). Breathe. Repeat. A variation would be to start with the legs in second position. When vertical, you can experiment with your balance by moving your legs forward and back and to the side independently from each other. Continue to breathe easily.

FIGURE 3-76

FIGURE 3-77

CONSTRUCTIVE REST STRETCH

This exercise is valuable as an aid to relaxation, breathing technique, and as a help in eliminating pelvic tilt, which is so prevalent among women. Do this one, in your own time.

1. Begin in the constructive rest position: lie on your back, knees bent toward the ceiling, feet flat on floor six inches to ten inches apart, arms crossed on the chest breathing easily, eyes closed, feeling the small of the back resting on the floor (see Figure 3–78). Lie in this position for at least thirty seconds to one minute before moving to the next step.
2. Gently slide the feet away from your body trying to keep the small of your back on the floor by using your abdominal muscles. Keep breathing.
3. When you have extended your legs all the way to the floor, draw them back up to the starting position, and repeat twice more.

Constructive rest is a position many dancers assume to give them maximum rest in the shortest time possible. In the twenty minutes between dance rehearsals I have heard dancers claim they have gathered what feels like an hour's rest by using constructive rest. So it is a useful passive exercise.

FIGURE 3-78   Constructive Rest

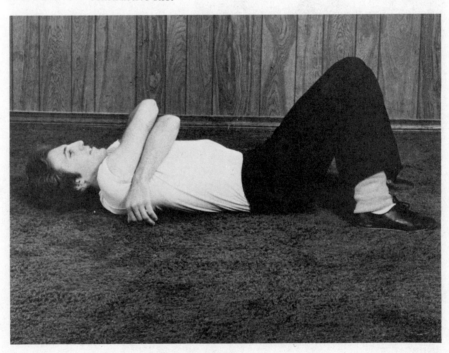

To achieve the desired goal of resting the small of the back on the floor, some women may have to draw their knees to their chest and hold them there easily with their hands. This is due to the natural shape of the female body and of the tendency in this society for women to stand with the pelvis tilted back. This can be an interesting character choice, but the actress should have the *choice*. So she should work to eliminate this particular quirk of alignment.

UP OVER EACH OTHER'S BACK

This exercise gives a stretch to the lower back and the inner thigh; it takes two people to perform.

1. Find someone with a similar body type and weight. Pair up with him or her, and sit on the floor back to back.
2. Person A places soles of feet together and links arms inside arms of Person B who has feet flat on the floor.
3. Person A pulls Person B up over back, as Person B pushes himself with feet into the final stretch position.
4. In the stretch position Person A is relaxed over forward, breathing easily, feeling the stretch created in the lower back and insides of the thighs, which is caused by Person B lying on his back on top. Person B's back should conform to the shape of Person A's back—they should be head to head, shoulder to shoulder, and Person B's hips should be resting on Person A's back.
5. After thirty seconds or so of relaxed stretch, Person A should rise up into a sitting position as Person B cooperates by coming down simultaneously into a sitting position.
6. Then they reverse roles, with Person A going up over Person B's back, Person A's feet are flat on the floor, while Person B has soles of feet together, legs relaxed out to side.
7. Each person does each part two times.

SEQUENTIAL SITTING UP
(FOR ABDOMINAL STRENGTH AND SPINE FLEXIBILITY)

1. Assume a supine position, small of the back on the floor, arms at the side, feet extended.
2. Sequentially sit up, leading with head and neck, upper, middle, lower back, until you are hanging over your feet—for eight counts.
3. Flex the feet and hang (relax into the position) for eight counts. Then stretch for eight counts. (Think of stretching from the

77

back, not the shoulders. Lengthen the muscles, and don't tighten them. Relax and feel the energy flow.)

4. Take the body down, making sure each part of the spine touches the floor, extending the feet on the way down—eight counts.

5. Repeat again. Then cut the counts in half, four counts for each part. Then halve the counts to two.

HEAD AND SPINE

1. Sit with the soles of the feet together; push through in the small of the back and sit up so that the back is in a straight line perpendicular to the floor (see Figures 3–79 and 3–80).

2. Rotate the head slowly to the right, back, left, and front—in eight counts.

3. Repeat to the left—eight counts.

4. Slowly round the back, for four counts, relaxing the spine (see Figure 3–81).

5. Hang into this position—four counts.

6. Shake out all the tension in the shoulders and neck—four counts.

7. Reach forward from the small of the back, arms out and reaching away from the body in an upward angle, shoulders down and the head in line with the spine. Think of stretching from the small of the back and of lengthening the body—four counts (see Figure 3–82).

8. Reach forward with the arms, take them up, and arch the back, then let the arms glide down alongside the body, palms on the floor (see Figure 3–83)—four counts.

9. Push through the pelvis toward the ceiling, letting the head relax back using four counts (see Figure 3–84).

10. Return to position 8 using four counts.

11. Lift the arms from the floor and contract in the abdominal area—four counts.

12. Push through from the small of the back and sit up straight (see Figure 3–80)—four counts.

13. Place the hands on the ankles and the elbows on the knees (rounding the back naturally together), and press the knees down to the floor (see Figures 3–85 and 3–86); for four counts, and release, for four counts. Repeat.

14. Repeat the entire exercise.

FIGURE 3-79

FIGURE 3-80

FIGURE 3-81

FIGURE 3-82

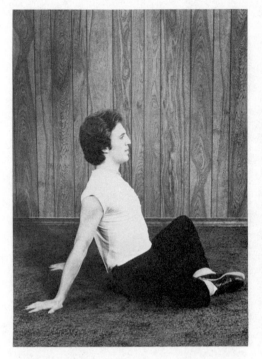

FIGURE 3-83

FIGURE 3-84

FIGURE 3-85

FIGURE 3-86

LEG UP AND STRETCH
(FOR KNEE AND ANKLE FLEXION)

1. Lie on your back, small of the back on the floor, legs parallel, feet pointed.

2. Bring the right knee up toward the chest, with both hands holding the underside of the thighs. The other leg stays extended—two counts. (Take the knee only as high as you can bring the lower part to meet it.)

3. Extend the lower part of the leg upward, foot pointed for two counts, and gently pull back on it stretching and lengthening—four counts.

4. Flex the foot and bend the knee slightly, two counts, and extend the foot and straighten the leg.

5. Take eight counts to bring the leg down slowly, leading with the toe, which is extended.

6. Repeat the same process with the left leg. Then repeat with each leg.

7. Then repeat with both legs simultaneously the same exercise, except you should take sixteen counts in lowering the legs. To keep the small of the back down press down in the abdominal area. Keep tension out of neck and shoulders.

KNEES INTO THE CHEST

1. Begin this exercise seated with the back straight and the knees drawn up to the chest, arms linked around the knees, feet flat on the floor (see Figure 3–87)

2. Place the arms out to the side of the body, parallel to the floor, and lift the feet off the floor extending your legs at a 45-degree angle to the floor, feet together. Keep the back straight, but allow it also to assume a 45-degree angle to the floor. You are now balanced in a V with only your buttocks on the floor (see Figure 3–88). Feet are pointed.

3. Flex the right foot toward you, both knees stay straight.

4. Point the right foot.

5. Flex the left foot as you did the right.

6. Point the left foot.

7. Repeat steps 3 through 6.

8. Flex both feet keeping the knees straight (see Figure 3–89).

9. Point both feet.

Knees into the Chest

FIGURE 3-87

FIGURE 3-88

10. Keeping the back straight and the toes pointed, bend both knees slightly so that the lower leg is parallel to the floor (see Figure 3–90).

11. Relax.

12. Now repeat steps 1 through 11 three times, trying to smile and breathe at the same time!

FIGURE 3-89

FIGURE 3-90

To teach this exercise, the arms, rather than extended to the side, may be used to prop up the back by placing the fingers of both hands on the floor behind you so that you have three points of contact (both hands and the buttocks) rather than one. Don't rush to get to the point at which you can balance without your hands. The object is to work the stomach and back muscles, not to perform a trick.

83

FLEX AND EXTEND
(FOR ANKLES AND KNEES)

1. Take a sitting position, legs extended, six inches apart and parallel, back straight, arms at the side (see Figure 3–91).

2. Flex the right foot and bend the knee at the same time (see Figure 3–92)—two counts. (Don't slide the heel on the floor.) Now extend the leg and the foot—two counts. (Think of extending all through the leg and out through the toes.)

3. Repeat the same sequence with the left foot. Then repeat, right, left.

4. Repeat with both feet, flexing and extending, four times.

5. Now gently take the body over the feet and hang—eight counts (see Figure 3–93).

6. Stretch toward the feet eight counts, reaching from the back (see Figure 3–94). (Stretch should be felt in the back and the back of the thighs).

7. Reach forward with the arms (see Figure 3–95), reach out, reach up (see Figure 3–96) arching the back (see Figure 3–97) and bring them down in a smooth circle, resting the weight on the elbows—four counts.

8. Slowly lift the right leg up, for four counts, foot extended, leg turned in (see Figure 3–98); flex the foot (see Figure 3–99) and slowly bring the leg down, for four counts, keeping it turned in. (Inhale as you lift the leg, exhale as you lower, and follow this breathing for the remainder of the exercise.)

9. Repeat the same process to the left.

10. Repeat right, left, but when legs are up, hold leg at ankle and stretch for four counts (see Figure 3–100).

11. Now lift both legs, for four counts, feet extended; flex the feet and lower, for four counts, but do not touch the floor. Repeat three more times. (Follow the breathing pattern.)

Flex
and
Extend

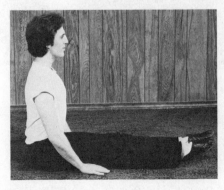

84   FIGURE 3-91   FIGURE 3-92

FIGURE 3-93

FIGURE 3-94

FIGURE 3-95

FIGURE 3-96

FIGURE 3-97

FIGURE 3-98

FIGURE 3-99

FIGURE 3-100

85

SECOND POSITION FLEX AND STRETCH
(FOR STRETCHING LEGS AND FEET)

1. Sit with legs in second position, with feet extended, knees pointing up to the ceiling, not rolling in, and sit squarely on the buttocks with the torso directly above. Place the right arm in front of the pelvis, and the left behind the buttocks, to help hold the position (see Figure 3–101).

2. Flex the right foot and bend the knee for two counts (see Figure 3–102), and then extend through the foot and leg—two counts. Don't let the heel slide along the floor; keep it stationary.

3. Repeat with the left leg. Repeat right and left.

Second Position Flex and Stretch

FIGURE 3-101

FIGURE 3-102

FIGURE 3-103

86

4. Do both legs at the same time, four times (see Figure 3–103).

5. Hang directly over both legs (see Figure 3–104)—eight counts. (Relax, do not stretch.) Then swing the body over to the right side and hang over the leg for eight counts (see Figure 3–105). Repeat to the left. (This helps you to relax the body for stretching.)

6. Now relax again forward and hold onto both ankles; gently stretch forward and down from the back, keeping thigh muscles relaxed and the pull even and steady. Think of the energy flowing out through the body.

7. Repeat steps 5 and 6 with both legs, this time taking hold of the ankle on the right (see Figure 3–106) and stretch gently for eight counts; then repeat to the left (see Figure 3–107).

FIGURE 3-104

FIGURE 3-105

FIGURE 3-106

FIGURE 3-107

BREATHING IN ON HANDS AND KNEES
(FOR RELAXATION AND ELASTICITY IN BACK,
AND FOR BREATHING TECHNIQUES)

1. Form a flat back with the hands and knees on the floor, arm extended straight, face looking at the floor.

2. Breathe in the eight counts as you arch your back sequentially up toward the ceiling, from the small of the back to the base of the head—focus on trying to fill the back with air.

3. Exhale in eight counts while sinking the spine sequentially toward the floor beginning again with the small of the back to the base of the head. (The face will look forward briefly as the neck begins to sink toward the floor, and then the face too in its turn will sink toward the floor as part of the sequential movement.)

4. Repeat in eight counts up and in; eight counts down and breathing out.

5. Repeat in four counts breathing in; four counts breathing out.

6. Repeat in two counts breathing in; two counts out.

STRETCH, SIT, PUSH THROUGH, AND SIT
(FOR STRETCH OF BACK AND STOMACH MUSCLES)

1. Begin with knees, chest, face, and arms on floor [in classic Middle Eastern prayer position] (see Figure 3–108).

2. Breathe in in four counts as you come to a kneeling position with arms at your sides, sitting on your lower legs (see Figure 3–109).

3. Breathe out in four counts as you put your hands on the floor behind you and push forward and upward as far as you can with your pelvis (see Figure 3–110).

4. Breathe in as you return to the sitting position, in four counts.

5. Breathe out as you return to original position, in four counts.

6. Repeat using four counts for each movement.

7. Repeat using two counts for each movement.

8. Repeat step 7.

FIGURE 3-108

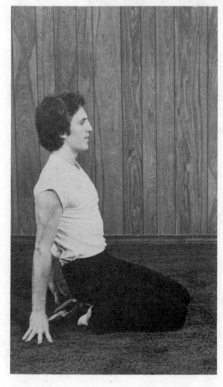

FIGURE 3-109

FIGURE 3-110

89

SIT, PUSH, SIT, ROLL
(UPPER BODY STRENGTH)

1. Lie in prone position, face down on floor, with hands under the shoulders, elbows poking up (see Figure 3–111).
2. Breathe in for four counts as you roll to your right (keeping the right hand on the floor but lifting the left hand) into a sitting position with right leg straight, left leg bent, knee toward the ceiling and foot flat on floor six inches to eight inches from right leg (see Figure 3–112).
3. Breathe out in four counts as you push your entire body off the floor and reach toward the ceiling with your left hand (thrusting your pelvis up as far as possible) while your right hand

Sit, Push, Sit, Roll/Arch and A

FIGURE 3-111

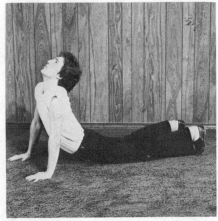

FIGURE 3-112

FIGURE 3-113

FIGURE 3-114

with straight right arm, left foot with bent left leg, and right foot with straight leg provide three points of contact with the floor, and lift (see Figure 3–113).

4. Breathe in for four counts as you sit back down.

5. Breathe out in four counts as you roll back to the starting position, with hands under shoulders.

6. Now repeat entire sequence to the left using four counts for each movement. This time the left leg stays straight, left hand remains on the floor, right hand lifts and extends, and right leg lifts over left and bends so that the right foot is placed flat on the floor.

7. Repeat entire exercise four times using only one count for each movement.

FIGURE 3-115

FIGURE 3-116

FIGURE 3-117

FIGURE 3-118

91

ARCH AND A EXERCISE
(FOR UPPER BODY STRENGTH)

1. Begin in the same position as preceding exercise—supine, hands under shoulders. Take a deep breath and exhale (see Figure 3–111).

2. Extend the arms straight out to their limit, while you breathe in, arch the back, and lift the face toward the ceiling in four counts (see Figure 3–114).

3. Lift the pelvis off the floor, keeping the legs straight, and lift the pelvis as high as you can so that the body forms an A position—while you breathe out in four counts (see Figure 3–115).

4. Lift the left foot off the floor and lift the leg and foot over the right leg as you pivot your body on your right hand and foot until your left hand also comes off the floor. Bend your left leg as you lift it up and over the right leg (see Figure 3–116) so that you can stop your rolling momentum by placing the sole of your left foot on the floor as you turn body and face toward the ceiling—all this as you breathe in in two counts.

5. Breathe out in four counts as you sit (see Figure 3–117).

6. Breathe in in four counts as you lift your pelvis toward the ceiling as far as you can, and reach your left hand toward ceiling (see Figure 3–113).

7. Breathe out in four counts as you sit again, bringing left arm down (see Figure 3–117).

8. Breathe in in four counts as you lift pelvis off the floor, kicking left leg up.

9. Pivot torso on right leg and hand, and catch yourself with your left hand as your body pivots toward original position (see Figure 3–118).

Bounce and Up

FIGURE 3-119   FIGURE 3-120   FIGURE 3-121

10. Breathe out as you lower left leg and torso back into original position in four counts.

11. Repeat to left side lifting right leg and hand, keeping same breathing technique.

12. Repeat right and left using one count for each movement—matching breath to movement.

13. Repeat right and left again, using one count per move.

As you can see this is a very advanced exercise and should not be taught when students are first learning technique and building their strength. But after some prior conditioning both men and women can gain much from this exercise. Men should go from this exercise immediately into push-ups as a further extension of the intended purpose—to build upper body strength.

BOUNCE, BOUNCE, AND UP

This exercise is for strengthening the hamstrings. *Caution:* Don't force things.

1. To find the start position, stand and place the feet in the parallel plié position, do a deep plié, then place the palms of your hands on the floor in front and outside of the toes, head up. This is the starting position (see Figure 3–119).

2. Do two slow bounces, followed by two quick bounces, then, slowly straighten the legs, keeping the hands on the floor (or as close as you can keep them) and the chest to the knees (see Figure 3–120).

3. Repeat three more times. On the last repetition, once you have straightened the legs, grasp the ankles and gently stretch your chest toward your legs for four counts (see Figure 3–121).

FIGURE 3-122

FIGURE 3-123

FIGURE 3-124

4. Then walk out with the hands (see Figures 3–122 and 3–123), keeping feet flat on the floor. Then walk the feet in (see Figure 3–124) to meet the hands. Grasp the ankles with both hands again and again stretch your chest toward your legs for four counts (see Figure 3–121). Slowly come up, through the spine, to a standing position.

ENDING THE WARMUP

FOOT FLEXIBILITY

This exercise is for foot articulation and prepares the student for jumps and leaps. It teaches the proper mechanics of jumping, rather like running the engine of a rocket while the rocket is tied down. In this case, your feet and legs are working as they would for a jump (only separately and not together as they will eventually need to) and your body is the

Foot Flexibility

FIGURE 3-125

rocket. In both cases the engine is warmed up and tested before using it to practically lift.

1. Assume first position with feet parallel and arms curved a bit, at the side.

2. Lift just the right heel and press the ball of the foot into the floor (see Figure 3–125), lower, repeat the lift, and lower three more times. Then repeat with the left foot.

3. Now lift the foot in three stages: heel (see Figure 3–125), ball (see Figure 3–126), toe (see Figure 3–127), and bring the foot back down onto the floor, toe, ball, heel. Do this four times on each foot.

4. Now keep the three stages in rapid lifts heel, ball, toe and lowering, toe, ball, heel, one count to come up, one down. Think of pushing the foot off the floor. Do not lift the hip.

FIGURE 3-126   FIGURE 3-127   95

JUMPS (FOR STRENGTH
AND CONDITIONING OF THE LEGS)

1. From the end position of the last exercise (in first position), do four demi-pliés (as a preparation for jumps) with a relevé between each plié, using one count for each movement (that is, plié down and straighten, relevé up, and down). Keep the flow of energy smooth and even just as in pliés so that the movement isn't start/stop or jerky, so that the muscles of the feet and legs work continually.

2. Instead of rising up into relevé on the last two counts, put on a burst of energy so that your feet rise off the floor in a small jump.

3. Continue these small jumps until you have done eight jumps in first position, and on the last jump move both legs into second and continue jumping in second position.

4. Then do four more jumps in first, and four more in second.

Make certain that you begin each jump in plié, and that you land in plié (or you will give yourself shin splints). Also make certain you extend your feet in the air so that your toes are pointing toward the floor, and that you land through your feet in succession: toe of the foot, ball of the foot, and finally the heel—there should not sound a large "thud" when you land, otherwise you will hurt your foot. Also these are *small* jumps. Invariably someone in my early classes takes this exercise to mean "Let's see how high you can jump!" This is not intended, it is discouraged; heroic efforts are out of place in any warmup. Serious dedication to mastering the essentials of centering, strength, and stretch is all that is required. One more note: Do not buckle in the waist, or lift in the shoulders—the feet and legs do all the work!

FRUSTRATION JUMPS (TO AID IN RELAXATION
AND EASE MENTAL STRAIN)

1. Begin in a low squat, legs turned out, hands on the floor between the legs.

2. Leap as high in the air as you can, raising your arms up, flailing the legs, and shouting out all your frustration.

3. Do three jumps in a row, allowing your body to collapse onto the floor at the end of the last jump, and relax.

This ends the exercise portion of the class with a note of frivolity and erases tension better than any other single technique I know of when combined with the following exercise.

BREATH RHYTHM

This exercise is usually done at the end of a warmup, after vigorous exercise. It helps return one to a relaxed, neutral state.

1. Take a supine position, feet parallel, arms loose at sides, and the small of the back on the floor. (If the back will not lie flat, don't strain; just bend knees and put soles on the floor.)

2. Talk or think yourself through the tension-draining process, or shake your tension out.

3. Once in a neutral state, concentrate on your breathing and try to find its rhythm. You will know when you have it.

4. With your breathing rhythm slowly rise to a standing position. Find the easiest way up, so you don't change or lose the rhythm. Rise in a fluid motion.

5. Once up, check on alignment. Is weight centered? Are legs pulled up? Knees relaxed? Muscles pulled across? Shoulders down? Back open? Neck and face relaxed? Test alignment by pressing up through feet and down.

COMMENTS AND SUGGESTIONS

To these suggested general exercises you will probably wish to add a good many more of your own choosing—certainly, more stretches, bounces, jumps, and certain calisthenics, especially push-ups. To include all the exercises one uses over a several-month period would triple the length of this section. Moreover, everyone has his needs, preferences, and special circumstances, and therefore I invite the student and the instructor to improvise and adapt, as the situation warrants, the rest of the general exercises.

Remember, however, to keep in mind these basic rules:

1. Warm up the entire body.
2. Understand the purpose and mechanics of the exercise.
3. Start simply and easily before any strenuous work.
4. Use your exercises to focus the day's work.

Also, keep one more thing in mind: This is a movement for actors class—not a dance class.

The exercises should be kept simple and the technique should be as consistent and undemanding on superfluous movement as possible. Sophisticated movements that demand a high degree of technical proficiency will close off actors to the classroom, instructor, and their bodies. It encourages competition and tension, and it decreases spontaneity and cooperation. The longer the class meets, the more proficient the students will become with the simple movements and the more readily will they respond as a group to additions such as complicated arm patterns and more difficult exercises.

4
EXPLORATIONS

- *Explorations of the Body: in Seven Phases*
- *Walks*
- *Music Improvisations*
- *Analysis: The Elements of Movement*
- *Space*
- *Space Explorations*
- *Essence-Study: Abstractions*
- *Gesture*
- *Haiku Exploration*
- *Action Verb*
- *Energy*
- *Physical Essence of Self*
- *Time*
- *Emotion*
- *Conclusion*

Exploration has always been the first step toward exploitation. This is no less true of stage movement study. Until the actor is aware of the full range and depths of his resources, how can he be expected to use them?

I have detailed in this area of study many of the more useful tools I have found for this exploration, organized in such a way as to provide the same type of progressional acquisition of skills detailed in the Exercises. Beginning with the most elementary (and necessary) explorations of the body, the student is led through several series of Explorations that demand (and hence, reveal) progressively deeper levels of intellectual and emotional awareness.

The seemingly random arrangement of the Exploration series, can only be rationalized once one understands the need to place the actor in a situation that is at once familiar and reassuring, and in which he feels capable and responsible for his own growing comprehensions. This is why many of the Explorations have the same starting sequence of instructions; and it is the reason for this particular sequence of Explorations. It is also the key to providing a relaxed and positive atmosphere free of competition.

Keep in mind that for all Explorations, discussion must *follow*, not precede, the action. Too much information and too many answers to too many questions provide false roadmaps to uncharted areas. In other words, too much prior discussion destroys the very process we are trying to stimulate. I don't let actors ask "How, What, Why, or Where from." They will be able to tell me once they have returned. If one or two go off on a tangent and learn something other than what I intended—so what? And if one or two feel as though they have learned nothing, it is not unusual or alarming—many times the puzzle looks like just a pile of pieces until it is assembled. Effort on one day may not be rewarded with brilliant success, and it is not daily reward students should be led to expect. Rather, it is over a period of time, after much serious study that awareness of progress can be detected. This is the attitude that must be encouraged.

This is why it is important that past and future efforts be organized and related as continually as possible, and why some of the material contained in this book may seem repetitious. Nothing encourages future effort more than success at past effort, and if we can ensure success (that is, reward) at one level, we can guarantee future effort at another.

The material contained in this chapter is the heart of my stage movement training because it awakens the actor to the many levels and manners of the mind–body connection. It is frivolous and irresponsible to propose (as some do) that an actor need only condition and sensitize his body. That is physical education, not stage movement training. Stage movement training should awaken the actor to the world of movement: pure movement, abstract movement, human movement and its motivations especially. It should help the actor understand how emotions affect the body; how physical states affect the mental processes; how imagery, memories, and suggestions affect the body through the unconscious layers of the mind. Actors are generally more sensitive to spatial relationships, time compression, and states of energy in themselves and those around them than are most people. Stage movement training seeks to awaken actors to their own sensitivity, to make them more aware and confident about the things they may subconsciously already know. Why? So that they then can exploit that knowledge more fully. Also, it serves to awaken in them new ways of seeing and experiencing to help them know more than they were capable of knowing before.

There is an odd fact associated with movement: While all movement is essentially nonverbal physicalization, it is also paradoxically invisible. Ordinarily we just do not see movement, do not consciously observe what we see, whether in our own movement or the movement in the world around us. Like the untutored witness to the crime who knows that someone shot someone else but is unable to say for certain which hand held the weapon, how many shots were fired, how long it took, or even whether a man or a woman did the deed—many times we are unable to "see" the movement of the world around us because we are so busy trying to understand it. "Explorations" help to materialize and make visible for study this world of movement. It is interesting to note that seeing the world more clearly may help the actor to better understand it. Explorations also help supply the guides with which we can chart this vast basically undiscovered world of movement.

The most useful guides are the basic concepts for all movement: space, time, and energy. All movement occurs in and occupies space; it is measured by time; and it requires energy to begin and complete itself. Space,Time, and Energy, then, provide the major frames for viewing this world. Throughout the Explorations these three frames focus the study. The stress falls on the interplay between the actor's intellectual grasp of the concepts and the growing visceral awareness of his body. Again, while the order in which the Explorations are presented has been consciously conceived for the most efficient learning, the order is not canonical; some revision, selection, and improvisation within the general framework, and a good many additions, are heartily recommended once the basic design is understood.

EXPLORATIONS OF THE BODY: IN SEVEN PHASES

Isolation of the Parts

This isolation work adds an awareness of motion to the already acquired discovery of segments of the anatomy.

Explore each area, limb, and structure of the body for its movement potential. Start with the head; rotate it, move it forward and back, side to side, vibrate with it, sway it, bounce it, get it moving every way you can imagine. (Always begin cautiously.)

Continue to discover all the movements you can with your arms, legs, feet, pelvis, torso, chest, even your elbow. Don't forget about all the muscles in your face.

Now build combinations. Add shoulder to arm, or add hand too, and a side of the torso.

Try isolated and combined explorations while stationary, while walking or ambling about, in different levels, prone, sitting, standing. Stay relaxed, open, and loose. Acquire the feel of all these movements.

Self-Contact and Sensations

Assuming a supine position on the floor, bring yourself to a neutral state by sapping the body of all its tension. You are going to be touching your body with three kinds of contact: slapping, tapping, and rubbing. (You may invent other kinds of touching on your own, preferably after you have explored these three.)

Once in a neutral state, you can move into any position that assists with the contact. But the progress of the contact should begin at the top of your head and move sequentially to your feet.The best way is to begin with one kind of touch and go over the whole body, starting by slapping head, ears, back of the neck, shoulders, all the way down to your ankles. Then run through with tapping, and so on. Try different intensities with a single touch—firm, light, sudden, slow, and so forth. Then mix up the three touches on a single area of the body: slap, tap, and scratch the thigh, and mix up the intensities.

When the class is emotionally prepared, this exploration can be performed by two actors. This exploration is also good for warming up the actor and develops relaxation techniques.

Movement Initiation

This Exploration studies how a movement begins in one part of the body and is extended by follow through into other physical segments.

Start with a simple hip rotation, moving only the hips. Then allow more and more of your body to follow the circular movement of the hips, with the hip rotation still clearly your focus so your total body is moving from a single source, the hips.

Then stop and renew simple hip rotation, but add on the thigh, then the whole leg, knee, calf, foot. This is the succession of movement, and you should move the focus of the movement down the leg as you gradually extend and enlarge the movement.

Once you grasp the principles, experiment with other parts of the body. The hip is easiest, but the head and the shoulder also work well.

Then explore how movement can originate in the center of the body, around the solar plexis, rib cage, and pelvis. Take head or limbs out from the center.

Motion Exploring

This Exploration employs some of the basic locomotor movements: walking, skipping, running, jumping, hopping, sliding, galloping, and so on. First, simply test and play with each of these locomotor styles, either in a random manner around the room or in lines of four actors abreast, in waves, across the floor, for clearer observation. Then build combinations, such as skip-jump-slide, or run-gallop-run-walk, or hop-slide-hop-slide. All this playing around is to develop a sense of freedom in moving about—freedom especially from the fear of moving, a fear developed from our loss of the variety of locomotor styles somewhere around early adolescence. This type of movement is distinct from dance combinations that require specific exacting "technique" that can inhibit rather than free an untrained actor's ability to feel and observe his body in motion.

Mirror Study*

The actors should pair off and face each other as though each is looking in a mirror. Initially one should be designated as the originator, the other as imitator. The two should be working to maintain the illusion that they are looking into a mirror. The action is imitation, and roles of originator and imitator should be exchanged. The originator should begin with an assortment of simple moves, gestures, twinges, twitches, and so on, avoiding movements that would force the imitator to turn his back to the originator. The imitator should try to become very quick and sure (and stay relaxed) with his copying, closing the time gap as much as possible. This exploration can take five to ten minutes for each originator the first time through. This technique can be returned to frequently over a year's study in order to reinforce observation, concentration, and sensitivity. Eventually the assignment of originator–imitator roles should no longer be necessary, as the actors learn to trust and understand each other, so that they are both originating and imitating simultaneously—and thus are spontaneously creating together. Actors skilled in this activity can remain focused and usefully involved for half an hour or more before tiring.

An advanced variation is the question and answer technique. Instead of copying, returning single movements, the point is to build an exchange, a set of signals and responses. The simple mirror work is needed to develop sensitivity to another's moves, as a prelude to answering. Make conversations: tell how you feel, what you are thinking about, what you are, what you want to do. But avoid close mime or code gesturing or charade language. Trust yourself to express the essence of what you are trying to say directly. This is very difficult work initially, but it does help acting students to get to know one another.

Blossoming and Withering†

Explore the body by trying on the analogy of a body being born, coming to life, rising, developing, extending, discovering powers, maturing, peaking, until fully "blossomed." Start prone, and slowly escalate your energy level as you go into whatever "blossoming" activity seems called

*Viola Spolin is usually credited with conceiving mirror exercises. See *Improvisation for the Theatre* (Evanston, IL: Northwestern University Press, 1963).

†This material is derived from Jerzy Grotowski, *Towards a Poor Theatre* (New York: Simon & Schuster, 1968).

for. Remain at the peak until it is fully explored. Then begin "withering." You slowly lose energy and the body slowly collapses. Don't rush this exploration.

The most important benefit of this process is the finding of the peak, feeling what it is like to be so vibrant and alive. The study also reinforces tension and relaxation exercises and heightens a general body awareness, while stimulating the imagination.

Facial Masks

Assume any posture or position you wish, one that reflects some kind of attitude, personality, or emotion. Now find a face that goes with the body's attitude. Know who you are, what you want, where you are going—all to sharpen your grasp of the attitude you are forming with your body. Move around in this posture, sharpening the sense of the reality of this attitude. You are starting with an external form, a cooly selected state of being, and by moving around in it, wearing the appropriate physical mask, you should begin to gain an internal sense of the attitude—the emotions and specific sensations of such an external bearing.

Once you have the feel of one attitude, select another, but this time start with a mask, a facial attitude, and then find the body to match the face. Now try to locate the "gut," the sensations of this attitude. Move around in this frame of body and mind until you feel comfortable with it and it begins to soak through you.

When everyone is secure in his selected identity, the whole class should attempt some rudimentary mingling, with individuals seeking to relate to one another from within identities. The directions cannot be explicit and predictive. The goal is a give and take openness to all the physical stimuli in mingling.

If the relating seems to be going smoothly, the whole class should come to a sudden freeze, one that crystallizes the identities. Each actor should study the person closest to him. Then slowly move in transition from his posture and attitude into the other person's: first the obvious physical configuration, the mask, and then unfreeze, move around, and try to pick up the inner feel. After another freeze the process should be extended.

Now reverse the process and begin with first fixing upon or creating an inner attitude. First, prone on the floor, regain a neutral state, drain out the tension and clear the head of the previous masks. Lying there, think about all kinds of identities, characters, moods, personalities, and select one to work with. Begin to take in or develop the feelings and thoughts of this identity, asking the same basic questions about it (that is, Who am I? What do I want? Where am I going?). Then assume this identity. You are still on the floor, only within you is the gut, the psyche, of this identity. Now, arise, reborn into another identity, and discover the facial mask, the appropriate body, the revealing movements.

This work involves primitive characterization. The study explores getting inside alien identities through two routes—starting from the outside, an external, technical route, and starting from a direct grasp of the inner condition, an internal psychological path. Both are frequently employed, and both are necessary for versatile acting. The point is to focus attention on the direction of flow. One direction is from physical expression toward inner form, the other is from inner form toward physical expression.

A Note on Observation and Imitation

If an actor's art largely consists of recreating other beings, movement studies offer an immediate and direct access to these other things. The classic technique for finding models for recreation is observation and imitation. What one sees, as he observes, is an amalgam of general types (old lady, soldier on leave, brisk businessman, smart-mouthed, street-wise kid, and so forth) and peculiar instances (the wino who humps along looking behind him, that suburban lady with the frank stare, and the little old lady who hums to herself and smiles in all directions). One can at first be blind to anything but the broadest types, or bewildered by unrepeated individual cases seemingly impossible to type. Observing the rich exchange between "type" and "individual" requires practice and work.

So, first one must learn to focus and structure his observing. Generalities and typological assertions are generally (sic) not to be trusted. Yet one can discover a surprising amount of truth in trying them on. Let us look at the old favorite—the comparison between the infant and the old man, two semi-hairless, physically feeble creatures, at opposite ends of life's linear advance. One can observe in any infant his precarious legs, unsteady balance, his free but slow arm gestures, and his curved but supple torso. In the old man there is likely a similar leg instability, another kind of torpid arm movement, and a sagging, curved torso. So far so good. But beyond these striking similarities are some painfully obvious differences. The elderly's hesitant and sharp gestures, the obvious fact that his torso seems to have been bent permanently into that curve, and his basic fragility, all contrast to the soft resiliency of the child's movement. There is enough truth in the comparison then, a sufficient analogy, to make a good, useful exercise from it. (Do old age and then do an infant, note similarities and differences, and so on.)

In the differences that close observation yields lie the most interesting discoveries. Special points of focus can produce new systems for typing. Look for different kinds of mouth movement, eye work, fingering, pelvis positioning, buttock swings, and so on. One observation technique is to watch necks one day, elbows the next, and so on. The closer one focuses the observation, the finer and more fascinating the data observed. It all depends on what you need to look for. A model for a businessman in a play? Types of running for a class exercise? You must be explicit in knowing what you are looking for, or else you will drown in types and particulars. A system of mental (or written) cataloging helps organize and retain the data. Immediate imitation is a sure way for strong retention. Copying the posture of the woman next to you on the bus may prove embarrassing, but getting it at once is necessary. A safer method is to follow your subject down the street—at a considerable distance, of course. Working in teams and comparing and checking versions also helps. Hopefully, something like a mental catalog of physical movement can be created and stored away for further use. A long and close observation and imitation session, such as with a mailman or police officer, who is exposed to daily scrutiny, can actually so involve you that you will develop a certain raw empathy with him, a kind of identification, not unlike what one does in developing and getting to know a character one is working on or getting into for a play. In a way, this phenomenon is rather like the basic activity of the "doubling" exercise in sensitivity training, wherein the members of the encounter group closely imitate one another in order to get a little better feel of what it is like to be in each other's shoes. Viola Spolin's mirror exercises can also establish this kind of raw empathy. But once he knows himself, the basic goal for an actor is to get outside himself, to discover other ways of being and moving.

WALKS

The simplest and least analyzed stage movement is the simple walk, yet it is usually the first movement an actor makes in a performance, and it tells the audience how far he has gone into his role. If he is the least ill at ease in his role, or still groping for the role's center, it is in the walk that he will give himself away.

Let us encourage a healthy and freeing self-consciousness toward walking. First, take the normal, customary walking style. The actor or the instructor should perform an analysis on it, noting all the peculiar mannerisms. It is helpful if the acting students analyze one another's walking as well. Of course, once the idiosyncrasies are pointed out, we must try to eliminate the more glaring problems, and this will take a number of sessions over some length of time. But the advance toward a "pure walk" (or some approximation) can be speeded up by experimenting with exaggerated walks: walking with extreme tension, like a mechanical monster or a stick man; with utter relaxation, almost collapsed, like a sloth or a monkey; with weight way back on the heels, always teetering on an invisible edge; weight slung forward; stylized mincing; deer-like loping. The list is long, but the point is that such experimenting with strange, exaggerated walks helps one feel how an ideal walk must be performed, reinforces alignment work, and should increase the range of styles at the actor's command.

An observation exercise will help these lessons to take hold. The acting students might go out into the streets, shops, and parking lots to observe many kinds of interesting walks. A useful way to structure the observation is to look for the different types of age grouping. One might start with a toddler, move up a few years for the next entry, and find characteristic samples of major age classes: young man or woman, middle age, and old age. The age classes are not really definitive, for social class and sex have their own walk imprint. Probably every environmental or psychological variable provides a unique addition to the age spectrum. So, try to deal with examples that strike you as representative. An interesting moment to capture is when a little girl begins to imitate how a woman walks.

A sample observation assignment might call for these walks and walking situations. A baby learning to walk; a child confronting a strange adult; a youth walking up to a member of the opposite sex; a middle-age person running for a bus, at work or on a lunch break; an elderly person walking across the street in rush hour or anxious to make it across before the light turns. Always use a specifically observed person in a specified situation, for example, a construction worker talking with his foreman, or eating his lunch watching females pass by on a sidewalk.

Then bring the persons observed into class and render their walks as faithfully as possible, trying always to communicate to classmates all that is specific about him or her (arthritis? just paid? walking in a drizzle?) and about the specific situation. If the renderings are successful, the lesson that emerges concerns just how much we can read of a person by his walking. The exploration also deepens the actor's ability to observe and draw from everyday experiences. It should also encourage a reluctance to generalize about movement styles. There is no such thing as the baby's walk or the old man's totter. In the specific texture of each person lies all that is interesting and important as resources for future acting. If some provocative class discussion fails to emerge from the exploration, consider it a disaster.

Walking Situations

Keep the characters you have discovered in your observations, for you are going to know and do them well enough in the first form to proceed to place them in new and different situations. This exploration is based on the quick demand for a specific new situation, activity, locale, and so on, and the actor's ready response. Usually a minute or two should be the maximum amount of time to think about it, for if the character's walk has been carefully learned, no more time is needed.

Here are some sample situations: going shopping on a rainy day without an umbrella; walking along a beach full of deeply browned sun bathers without a tan of your own; walking along and building up confidence for some challenge ahead; walking into a party full of strangers; walking away from a street fight you observed; walking home from work on a dark, November day; walking through a grocery store at peak shopping hours; walking by a cop just after you have jaywalked and you aren't certain whether he noticed or cares, and so on. In making up your own situations, you should try for those that have their own kind of implied drama, tension, and conflict.

MUSIC IMPROVISATIONS

This improvisation is an ideal change of pace, useful several times during the course of study, when free, opening, work is needed to refresh the actors from working within restricted, other-oriented projects, such as the observation series. It also helps to create a sense of ensemble in the class.

The exploration is based on a preselection of different kinds of music with different and interesting textures and feeling tones. The action of the exploration consists of listening and absorbing a piece of music, and then responding to the music physically. This is not illustrating music; rather, the point is to allow the music to drive one toward a certain kind of physical expression and response, shaping and communicating the essence of what the music makes you feel or think.

Start off relaxed, on the floor, in a neutral state. Lights may be dimmed. Then, let the music take over. At the end of the music, follow through with your actions until you have resolved that emotion or image; then, relax back on to the floor and allow the images, impressions, and tensions to drain away from you. Find your natural breath rhythm. When you are back to a neutral state, sit or stand up. Often lively discussion will follow. Sometimes an interesting single recording or composition works well. A tape of various pieces also works and provides for more stimuli.

Many different types of music can be used for this purpose such as nonvocalized rock compositions such as "Echos" from the Pink Floyd album *Meddle;* or sophisticated musical theatre scores, such as one side from *Leonard Bernstein Conducts his Music for the Theatre* on Columbia Records Masterworks Series; jazz recordings such as one side of Yusef Lateef's *A-flat, G-flat and C* on the Impulse label; Ira Gershwin's *Rhapsody in Blue* or *An American in Paris*, although perhaps too well known, have enough different levels for an interesting experiment.

Music from ballets such as Prokofiev's *Romeo and Juliet* can be used as long as the passages are not too didactically balletic to be sources for pure nonintellectualized movement. The key to selecting music for the musical improvisation is not to have a too specific spoken message (that is, "I wanna dance, dance, dance, Boogie you can dance" or "Hold me in your arms and tell me that you care," and so on), nor a too specific cultural interpretation to be taken out of context (that is, popular or even well-known popular classics, such as theme music from James Bond films or from *Doctor Zhivago*). The music should be a surprise to most of the participants (to say all would be asking too much), have clear and universal messages, and changes either inherent in the compositions themselves or built into the selection and arrangement of the varioius compositions recorded for the purpose.

Selection and arrangement of compositions can greatly aid the students toward understanding of the various units covered. Thus this single concept can be adapted so that there are an unlimited number of adaptations for this exploration, and it fits in well with space, time, and emotion explorations. (See Chapter 6, Practical Applications, for an illustration of musical improvisation.)

ANALYSIS: THE ELEMENTS OF MOVEMENT

Whereas the vocabulary of anatomical parts allows us to say precisely what in our body we are moving, and so refines our perceptions considerably (lower leg, middle back, rib cage, and so on), we still need the further refinement of perception provided by the basic terms of pure movement itself. We need to describe movement in terms of where, when, and how the body is moving—in other words, we must employ the perceptual frames of Space, Time, and Energy. Again, we must sound the theme of this study: Because physical expression and physical movement are little observed, noted, seen, and understood, because except for some athletes, artists, and dancers, no one is accustomed to seeing the movement and motion he is looking at, we must emphasize how we begin to see. Our first need is a language with terms and classes for movement that will organize what we see, and so allow us to see. Rudolf Laban was about the first to systematize this language, with his meticulous graphing of exact and minute combinations of Space,Time, and Energy. His disciples proceeded to organize this system in detail and have provided history with Labanotation, a detailed symbolic language of its own for seeing and recording explicitly all the movements in a dance. In stage movement training we do not need such an elaborate system. We only need the basic terms—Space, Time, and Energy—and an understanding of the primary elements that compose each basic term. The intent of the following explorations is to wed the anatomical movement vocabulary to the pure movement terms, both intellectually and kinetically. They will also provide a transition into the third level of mental awareness—emotions.*

SPACE

Let us first analyze space. The most basic feature of our environment is the physical space we occupy, and which in turn, occupies us. Space is around us, it is inside us. We move through space and space moves through us. Space is extremely flexible in that we can make it appear or disappear by the way we move through it. We have feelings about ourselves in space. We are sensitive to people and objects outside ourselves in space. We develop a response to other people's use of space and its effect on us. The way in which we relate to space is an important part of our expressive behavior.

We can best conceive of space through these frequently cited subcategories: direction, range, level, design, and focus. Direction characterizes the path of movement, whether forward, back, diagonal, circular, curved, or zig zag. Range indicates the amount of space used. Level tells us the altitude of the movement, standing, sitting, or lying down. Design, a more ambiguous concept, tries to communicate the whole pattern of movement, stationary and locomotor, both in terms of one body and a group of bodies and the shapes that they make. Focus designates the point to which the attention of the viewer is drawn.

SPACE EXPLORATIONS

A General Space Improvisation†

In the warmup for this exploration it helps if attention is called to the elements of space and how space is used in the exercises. Specific space exercises may also be devised.

*Thorough discussion of all three of these elements does not immediately follow because in the developmental process I am concerned with, other primary elements are necessary to explore between these basic levels of study. Space, therefore, follows this discussion immediately from pages 111–15; Energy is dealt with on pages 126–40; and Time is dealt with on pages 140–48. In introducing any one of these principle elements to my classes, I reinforce the concept that they are all essential to movement and will eventually be discussed and analyzed as they relate to each other, but in the early stages they must be dealt with individually (contrary to the Laban method) or the actor will simply get confused or feel that the material is too esoteric for serious consideration. A time interval between each section of study of these principle elements, then, helps the student and teacher alike to focus more finely on the pieces of the puzzle.

†The instructor must talk the students through this.

Begin in supine position, with eyes closed and the body in a neutral state, that is, mind cleared and tension drained. The instructor guides the student through the improvisation. First, become aware of the body in space, the space it occupies and the space surrounding it. Don't touch or move the body; just feel it in space and its relationship to others in the room, the space all around and the space inside you. Feel the head in space; feel the rest of the body and its space—again, without touching it. Feel what it would be like to move in space, but do not move. Imagine the sensations of your hand moving through space but do not move it.

Now begin to move the body in space. First in isolation, such as moving just the hand. Then go through the rest of the body in the same way, adding parts, and eventually, working up to the entire body in motion. Then, as you are increasing the movement, sitting up, standing, begin to become conscious of the levels of space, the directions, the range, the shape, and designs.

Once in a standing position, sense the different sensations of stationary movement and locomotor movement. Try to float through space and feel its lightness. Try shaping space with your body, soak it up, touch it, pat it, slice it, mold it into a ball, hug it, feel its texture and sense your body in it. Penetrate space with your body, push it, and so forth.

Now turn to an exploration in making shapes, designs, patterns with space and the body. After a while, each actor should become more aware of the other shapes in the room, and begin some reciprocal shape-influencing. Continue this improvised reacting. Then, without warning, everyone will freeze in his shape, upon command. Then a brief study of the frozen state: the shape of one's own body, how it relates to the total design of the room, how it relates to specific other spatial shapes. Now unfreeze and complete (follow through with) the movement patterns.

Place yourselves at random in the room. Now begin to walk toward someone in the room. Now move away from someone. Around. Through. Over. With. Against. Now touch the environment with as much of your body as you can. Slither, crawl, roll. Now stand and close your eyes, and begin to move around the room, but try not to touch anyone. Use your other senses to feel people near you, to feel all the space you are moving through. If you collide with a person or object, you must identify that object or person with your eyes still closed, and then move on. After a while, the command to freeze again begins another study period, eyes still closed. Then try to identify where you are, who is near by, what the room now looks like.

This exploration offers a great opening-up experience to the element of space and may be returned to later.

Shapes in Space

This is an Exploration of two principles of design: symmetry and balance and their opposites.

Begin with individual explorations of balanced movements, on all levels, stationary and locomotor, in various ranges. Here is a useful way to begin: Imagine the body cut in two on a vertical plane, thus creating two halves to be balanced or unbalanced. Stay balanced, even in transitions from sitting to standing. This is not weight balance, but design balance. You will note how difficult it is to hold a balanced design, since most moving requires a symmetrical–asymmetrical flow. You will also probably find holding a balanced design boring.

Now move to easier, more normal, unbalanced, asymmetrical designs. Note the increased amount of freedom in moving. After a while turn to an exploration of both balanced and unbalanced designs; work individually, then in groups.

Filling in Space

Pair off, one becomes A, the other B. The typical pattern has A make a shape with his body, then B relates to that shape by fitting into the enclosed space so created. As B fills that space, A then fits himself into the open space B has just created. Then B responds, then A, and so the process goes on, until exhausted or too tangled to proceed.

After a while pairs should pair off, so the pattern becomes an A-B-C-D sequence. Eventually the entire class should be joined into a chain of filling responses, a single, long, flowing, moving sculpture from A to Z.

Direction, Level, and Range

In the warmup for the day, pay attention to these three qualities of space in the selected exercises. Note the range factor from a demi-plié and to a grand-plié or the levels in jumping.

For Direction, the class should freely explore all the different directions the body can take, moving across the floor or standing still: take four steps forward, four on right diagonal, four to the left, and so on.

For Levels, working with falls is excellent. But remember it is wise to work with gymnastic mats or mattresses, in the early work especially. First do a knee fall—a continuous fall—a bit to one side with one arm out to catch the weight, starting with knees on the floor. Then repeat the process from a standing position. Then a walking fall, a trip or a slip, or being clubbed from behind, shot from the front, and so on.

For Range, a set of basic folk dances makes the exploration fun and culturally informative. In performing the Korabuska, the Teton Mountain Stomp, or the Miserlou, a rich assortment of range is evident. Ballroom dancing works equally well. [See Jane A. Harris, Anne Pittman, and Marlys S. Waller, *Dance A While: Handbook of Folk, Square,*

and Social Dance, 3rd ed., (Minneapolis: Burgess Publishing Co., 1967.]
The steps of any dance yield useful range and direction experience.

The sum of activities to develop Range, Direction, and Levels awareness is enormous. Be creative.

Spatial Relationships

Pair off and invent a specified relationship (mother–daughter, brother–sister, boss–employee) and then set up a situation (confrontation, lovers' quarrel, firing, celebration). Then, with the situation set, lie on the floor, clear the body, and in a neutral state think out the situation you developed. When ready—when the internal aspect of the role and situation becomes felt—get up and begin to move around in this situation. Relate and react to one another, not miming, but reflecting the essence of what you feel.

Now clarify the relationship but not the situation (that is, establish roles such as lovers, friends, parent and child—but avoid pat situations such as an argument, philosophizing over drinks, or comforting one another at a funeral). Let the situation evolve out of the movement; be sensitive to how the other person seems to feel his role. (For example, a mother may be anxious, bitter, or frustrated—there are all kinds of mothers.)

For both explorations, while inside your role try to note how the spatial relationship changes, depending upon the course of the interaction.

Gatherings

Invent any specific kind of gathering or group affair—from a family picnic, a class reunion, a town meeting, a crowded elevator, or a group of customers in a pornography shop, to witnesses at a fatal accident. What is important is that within this agreed on situation, each actor assume a *particular* role, character, or personality type.

There are two variations.

1. In a gathering of strangers, each person keeps his identity to himself, except as he reveals it in his movement and his spatial signature.

2. In a gathering of acquaintances or intimates, all identities are known (perhaps assigned) and are important to the spatial drama. It is necessary that Aunt Clara know who her niece Bess is.

3. There is actually a third variation, in which individuals take turns being ghosts, invisible nonpersons who float through the

gathering, able to observe without worrying about performing in his own space.

The point of the Exploration is to observe spatial relationships without overly intellectualizing them. Observe yourself. You should be able to easily observe your consciousness and unconscious use of space that arises from your understanding of the role and the situation. It should be quite exciting to observe the dimensions and patterns in all the contacts your character has in the gathering.

Before beginning, work into the identity as you did in "Spatial Relationships." At the end, have a long and detailed discussion.

This Exploration might be returned to later after the Abstractions work, to try the same activity with the abstracted essence of identities.

ESSENCE-STUDY: ABSTRACTIONS

Essence study: Seizing on the essence of something, capturing the epitome of an emotion or thought or gesture, getting into the center, passing through external barriers that either reflect or disguise the center. By seeking the "essence" of a physical or mental occurrence the student is forced away from the literal contexts and the outer form of the episode into an "abstraction" of the elements so that he can see its universal or essential qualities.

The act of "abstracting" here stands at the opposite end of the spectrum from the imitation of physical mannerisms in literal detail. We are trying to get through the outer trappings, into an intimate grasp of the inner nature of experience. In physical movement, gesture, and expression, "abstraction" is not an enlargement any more than it is a duplication. The essence of a handshake, for example, is not larger, more sweeping swings of the hand. That is merely blowing it up. To get at the handshake's essence, the best thing to do is to transfer the movement from the hand to another body part, say the foot, or into the whole body. Thus, the foot has a better chance of abstracting a handshake than the hand, since there is less danger of simply exaggerating. This is not the beginning of surreal (or flakey) exercises for a stylized, perhaps expressionistic, acting style. This is rather the beginning of the most serious and potentially most rewarding portion of movement study. One reason this Exploration is useful is that it helps the student to break down his preconceptions. It helps him understand in an immediate sense that familiarity with a thing is not the same as knowing it. By forcing the actor to abstract simple movements I force him to study his kinesthetic awareness of the movement as well as the meaning implicit in it. Any kind of acting requires this kind of penetration of externals that essence studies provide.

In all the work that has preceded this portion of study, there have been several guiding principles that essence studies help to focus for the student and teacher alike. First among these principles is the concept of organic movement. This simply means movement that flows naturally from the organic unity of the mind and body. In all that has been presented thus far we have been involved with aiding the actor to understand and trust this organic unity with the ultimate design of providing him with the tools to use the understanding of his truth to aid him in his acting assignments.

The Essence Study is both teaching aid and tool for the actor. By striving to master the subtle intellectual puzzle it presents, the student will awaken new pathways to his own psyche. Once conquered, the Essence Study becomes a valuable psychophysical tool to unlock the secrets of the character's inner reality. This is important because what we are ultimately doing is aiding the actor to convince an audience they are observing the organic reality of that character, and not to aid him to "wow them" with his virtuosic performance.

First things first, however. Let's start by focusing on the thing the actor must know first, and best—himself. To help the actor to do this we continue to do what we've been doing all along: We take away the actor's personal props. In the initial stages we were (and continue to be) involved in removing the actor's personal physical quirks (that is, the slouches, poses, tensions, bad breathing techniques, and other highly identifying personal movement traits) that would inevitably prevent the actor from assuming any role but his own on stage. With this later period of study we are attacking the actor's mental props (that is, those subconscious assumptions that support all our daily activities).

The reason we do this is that, although assumptions are useful tools to a reasoning and highly adaptive social animal (such as man, for instance), they are very often taken for fact by the mind that formed them. This is misleading to the performing artist, because *assumption of fact* is not the same thing as the *knowledge of fact*. If the artist does not know the difference between assumption and knowledge of fact, how can he be expected to breathe life into a character he is assuming?

The Essence Studies require the actor to *know* the facts. If he does not know before he begins the study he is involved with, he will discover it in solving the problem for him. Therein lies the usefulness of the Essence Studies: They aid in the discovery or revelation of the truth.

To understand as an informed reader where this mode of study is leading, it should be pointed out that the Essence Studies will be used in almost every succeeding element of study. For analysis of energy, emotion, intention, time, and many other topics, Essence Studies will aid the student in focusing on each individual concept by freeing him from the need to relate each term to a specific realistic situation. This allows the student to explore with mind and body in a more open manner, while maintaining a feeling of being firmly grounded in an intelligible and intelligently organized system of study.

In fact, that is what this is—an intelligently organized *system* of study. It is no mere coincidence that Essence Studies are introduced at this time. If the students have been assiduously applying themselves to the program thus far detailed, they are now ready to move into a more challenging and thought-provoking—and more creative—area of study. And the best place to start is in an area of focus they are already dealing with—their own bodies.

The easiest and most revealing way to approach the Essence Studies is to begin by using them to help analyze gestures. And the best way to begin is by comparing the results of an external method versus an internal method.

INTRODUCTION: ESSENCE/GESTURE

1. Try first the externally derived essence of wringing your hands. Wring your hands. Watch them as they move. Try to find what is essential to the movement. What makes the movement what it is? When you have found it, try to abstract that essential quality, giving the essence of the movement by moving another body part or parts. Do not settle for the first movement that pops into your mind and body; experiment with different movements until you feel you have grasped the essence of the original movement in at least three abstractions of it.

2. Now empty your mind and body. Come to a neutral position and breathe deeply in and out several times. Clear yourself of all unnecessary tension and relax. Now try to find or create within yourself a situation in which you did, or most probably would, wring your hands. Do not do the gesture until you feel you must, or until you feel it will help to understand the emotion. When you feel the wringing to be part of the situation, to be essential to your problem, see if you can find the universal or essential qualities of the episode. Try then to abstract it. Find the essence of this. Change both the emotion and the feeling that the movement is an integral part of the emotion. When you have done this, relax. Clear yourself. Breathe deep.

3. If you committed yourself to the task both times, you probably found different essences for what amounted to the same gesture. This is normal. Why? Because of the different approaches. You may feel one approach may have worked better for you than the other, or that both revealed something different, but worked equally well (or that neither approach had any effect). Whatever you discover will almost certainly be unique to you. But remember this is only the first crude step on a very elemental level. Immediate or profound results are not expected, and complete comprehension of either the benefit,

concept, or goal of these Essence Studies is impossible. All that is important for you to do at this stage is to commit yourself to each one you do fully. These questions you have will all be answered by your own effort.

Discussion

A reminder: *Which* gesture one uses and *when* one uses it are stage business concerns, best handled by the actor and the director in rehearsal. Here we are concerned with developing some experience in the origins of gesturing, and especially how gestures are performed. Of course the primary *how* is answered by these principles: precision, sequence, and clarity. Whatever the gesture and however derived, the audience must see it clearly. On stage one can exaggerate and enlarge a gesture, but except in certain comedy or camp melodrama, this broadening creates a false, stagey effect. Slowing it down slightly increases the visibility more than enlarging it. Breaking a gesture down into its component, smaller moves, helps one get that slowness without a lethargic slow-motion look to it. It also insures the precision. (For instance, you can think of lighting another's cigarette in four steps: hand to pocket, pull lighter out, bring it up to the cigarette, and flick for flame.)

The full meaning of "how" a gesture is performed leads us into observation studies, psychology, anthropology, and characterization. What are gestures? They are not the units in the special language of mime; nor are they the elaborate punctuation of stage speech. They are fairly specific actions of the body, often surrounded with over signification or indirect revelation, and occur in everyday intercourse.

Gestural Categories

Here are some of the major categories I work with in analyzing gestures:

1. *Functional gestures*—achieve a simple specific purpose. (*Examples:* combing your hair; scratching where you itch; looking at your wristwatch to check the time; brushing your teeth, etc.)

2. *Conventional gestures*—substitutes an unreflected movement for speech. (*Examples:* a nod = "yes"; shaking your head = "no"; raising the eyebrows = "oh?"; hunching the shoulders = "I don't know" or "What can you do?" or "Who cares?"; etc.)

3. *Social gestures*—ritualistic communications between members of the same gestural code, the same society. Some seem almost universal (*Examples:* waving "hello" or "good-bye"; putting one hand straight up at face height, palm facing another person to

mean "listen" or "quiet"; etc.), but there are many social gestures not generally understood between one society and another or even between one generation and another. (*Example:* American youth of the 1940s used the "V for Victory" to signal their desire and commitment to end their war with armed victory over their enemy, whereas their children used the same gestural signal to mean something far different. Initially, the parents were confused, and even with comprehension mutual understanding of the gesture was not universal.)

4. *Function gestures*—repeated unconscious routines. (*Examples: nonfunctional* licking of the lips; twitching of the face muscles; cracking your knuckles; drumming fingers on the table over and over again; chewing gum; etc.) *Note:* Many of these gestures are those that tend to annoy a second party when performed for a prolonged period in close confinement.

5. *Emotional gestures*—often replace language when verbalization is impossible or not needed. (*Examples:* holding hands; raising a fist; a kiss; a bear hug; opening the hands in shock or surprise, etc.)

6. *Shadow gestures*—may accompany language, may just be silent, but are unverbalized expressions of inner emotional activity not necessarily intended to be communicated. (*Examples:* a young boy's squirming in the chair while waiting in the principal's office; nailbiting; wringing of the hands; hunching the shoulders up and ducking the head; etc.)

The purpose of this classification is only to enlarge the awareness of the kinds of gesture one has to work with. There are probably a number of ways to classify gestures; this is not intended to be the last word on categories of gestures. But to help students understand some differences between one gesture and another, it is helpful to establish some of the different causes, motivations, and origins of the various body movements we call gesture. It helps them, then, to focus on a specific range of meaning for each study rather than to attack the subject on the broad front.

Each gesture that we do takes on meaning by the timing and manner of our performance. A nod can mean anything from "I am happy to see you alive today" to "I fully intend to destroy you if I can," and it is in most cases a conventional gesture. A nod can be a function gesture (in the case of a person who simply nods all the time for no visible reason); it may be a shadow gesture (in the case of a person awaiting trial nodding to keep their spirits from lagging); it may even be a functional gesture (as in the case of a person trying to stay awake during a lecture).

Any kind of gesture can be performed consciously or unconsciously, reflexively or nonreflexively. A "shadow gesture," for example, probably arises both reflexively and unconsciously, but one can also manipulate

119

gestures. In fact, most people manipulate their gestures automatically through the course of the day as situations change so that a person can play with their twitch of consternation to make it into a conscious sign the receiver will properly read as "beware." One can generally predict an intimate's gestures, they become so familiar and consistent. Yet they do vary as we might expect, from situation to situation. For example, at home a John Q. Smith may employ medium-range gestures in a straightforward manner, whereas in his office they may grow large and percussive; but when he consults his auto mechanic, they may become little and tentative. There are no firm rules for analysis. The point of this exercise is to savor the fascinating variety and nuance of gesture.

In terms of a gesture's meaning we must consider its psychological sources. Broadly, we can distinguish two courses: the desire to express and the need to conceal expression. In peak moments of elation, ecstasy, rage, horror, our gestures unfailingly give our inner state away by their direct, unpremeditated execution. When "our heart goes out to" someone, very likely our arms do too, revealing a natural flow of feeling outward. Here the gesture arises in our desire to express (push out, via gesture) what we are feeling or thinking. Yet conditioned as we are by social instruction and social experience not to feel things too intensely, at least not to show our feelings, we as frequently use our gestures to hide our feelings. We are not just considering situations where one of our hands cover a yawn or expression of shock, or serves to hide our tears. Rather, I am talking about all the gesture activity that creates and maintains our social mask. Partly this is our public face, the one we don in elevators, with sales clerks, and to anyone who seems to be pointing at us or talking about us in our presence. But the major feature of the social mask is its presence in even very private or intimate contacts. Immobility, a stonewalling of intrusions and expressions has long been almost a cultural ideal in many civilizations and cultures including modern Western social behavior.

Yet it is misleading to simplify the two sources into true and false categories. Our inner, real, true insecurity, for example, frequently produces false, protective, and immobile masks. So the outer face, although frozen, is not a false, merely external gesture, because freezing expression is an accepted protection. Generally it is true that our social and external masks keep us apart (even our sexy neighbor with the permanent smile of hello is really keeping his or her distance) while our gestures from within do reach out and establish contact with others, whether in anger or compassion.

This discussion is not to set up specific acting projects or movement explorations. In part it is meant to confuse, that is, to illustrate the inherent complications in studying gestural phenomena—all the rich, fascinating particulars and the problems in theorizing about them. For example, the common distinction between gesture and words: Actions have always been thought the truer expression, but we all recall times when our words spoke more accurately than our gestures. There are other occasions when gestures may be in conflict with one another—one betraying an inner desire (hands groping or patting), the other a social pose (body erect and face expressionless). Then there are less dramatic contrasts, such as an apparently relaxed slouch, legs casually crossed, foot slowly swinging, while the fingers tap out a staccato impatience on the end table. There are obvious exercises, explorations, and acting projects galore in this material, but perhaps the most useful way of dealing with the world as a swirl of gestures is to try to feel the truth and appropriateness in all the experiments you do with them.

Gesture Explorations

FUNCTIONAL GESTURE

1. Do a functional gesture. (Scratch an itch, comb your hair, pull up your socks, adjust your shirt, fold up the cuff on your shirt sleeve, or some other functional gesture.) Do not mime it. Do not, for instance, "pretend" you are brushing your teeth (if you have no toothbrush) or opening a door (when there is no door to open).

2. Observe the movement from the outside, and then try to feel what you are doing from the inside. Do it several times, each time observing from a different perspective until you understand it.

3. Once you feel you thoroughly understand it mentally and kinetically (how it feels to actually do the movement), experiment with different movements that embody the Essence of that understanding.

4. One by one present your studies to the class. Each person will do the gesture they have selected, and then present its Essence. Each person will do the Essence several times using different combinations of movements which carry the Essence of the original gesture. (One set of movements may feel or appear to most embody the Essence, but to keep everyone from settling for easy answers, I demand more than one Essence.)

The discussion for this exploration should focus on whether the movements discovered by each participant carried the same sense of purpose or bore any relationship to the original gesture. Oddly enough, even in these initial stages students will find it fairly obvious which people have understood and succeeded in presenting the Essence of their gesture. The same sort of mental and physical tensions are involved after all (though displaced to other body parts or reorganized temporally), and by the very commitment to comprehend, any serious student will be able at least to transpose the superficial realities of the simple movements involved.

Other topics of discussion should touch on the desirability of movement that has follow-through (actors should never be allowed to just drop off movement in the middle of a phrase), and that seems to come from the center. This should not be an important part of the discussion, but gentle reinforcement in a wide variety of activities will help to insure comprehension and appreciation.

CONVENTIONAL GESTURE

1. Do at least five different conventional gestures. (Shake your head "no" or "yes"; Say "I don't know"; "Go away"; "Get away from me"; "Come here"; "What did you say?"; each without any verbal utterance.)

2. Choose one of these and, as with the functional gesture, execute the movement several times, looking at it in different ways (what does it feel like; how much tension is involved, and where; what does it look like, etc.) until you understand it.

3. Find the Essence of this gesture. Try to find different qualities that may, at first, have been hidden from you by refusing to settle for the easy answer. Ask yourself "What is there in this gesture that I haven't noticed already?"

4. Again each person will present their studies to the class. Start with the movements you feel *most* embody the Essence of the original gesture. Do the Essence twice, then do the gesture. Finally, repeat the Essence.

After each presentation (which includes the Essence done twice, the gesture, and the Essence again), discussion of the ability or the inability to find the Essence will be followed by that person (whether or not the class felt they captured the Essence) presenting at least two movement sequences they have rejected in favor of the sequence presented. In this way the entire class will have the benefit of having their choices and efforts discussed openly in the same terms. The teacher or leader must keep the discussion in firm control and focused firmly on the goal; that is, helping each individual to come to an understanding of the value, purpose, and meaning of the Essence studies, especially as a tool to reveal the true nature of the (in this case) gesture.

Any number of gesture explorations can be devised and each should be useful. Gesture assignments encourage follow-through improvement, help to get movement started from the center, underscore the effectiveness of a few movements well done (the economy principle that helps one cut down on wild gestural flailing), and of course, are valuable practice and research for characterization.

Fragments/Follow-Through

The purpose of this Exploration is to teach follow-through in physical movement. But we will approach follow-through by comparing it to its opposite—fragmented movement—which is interrupted, incomplete, contextless movement.

1. Begin by creating and moving around in jerky, percussive fragments. Do this alone and do the fragments as though relating to other people. There should be no completion of a fragment nor any transition between fragments.

2. Now do movements in which you are thinking of the natural follow-through and completion. Try for a smooth flow in which all your movement phrases join a larger line that continues from the beginning to the end of the experiment.

3. After working alone on both fragments and follow-through, work with a partner, by making a movement conversation in which you talk in both fragmented and complete movement phrases. You are working on the essence of a conversation (not indicating or signaling), which is of course an abstraction exercise.

Note: When some clear communication has you readied, slowly ease into a transition toward a realistic conversation with everyday gestures, and you actually begin to verbalize, to converse, with each other. This is a subtle transition. Complete our silent, abstract conversation—don't break your conversation—but do work together toward the easy and natural drift toward conventional gesture and speech. You should feel the sense of follow-through in this very process.

4. A take-home assignment: Take a sentence or two from the dialogue of a scene you are already working on, perhaps a troublesome passage. Prepare an abstraction of those lines, the essence of the movement that underlies the verbalization, and be ready to do that movement with the words. Also prepare a conventional and realistic version. In class both will be performed. By working with but a brief passage we enjoy the greatest opportunity to get the words and the movement to flow together, one to follow from the other. Having dipped into the essence of the situation, the actor should have a firm inward grasp of the words and realistic movements that flow out from the center.

HAIKU EXPLORATION

This exploration prompts the student's creativity and reinforces work in abstraction. The "haiku" is a special form of Japanese poetry: very terse (three lines, seventeen syllables) yet highly patterned (five syllables in the first and third lines, seven in the second); it is also a dramatic form of poetry, with each line often taking a sharp turn in idea, with a minimum of explanatory transition. Thus the haiku offers a series of empty spaces to be filled in by the reader's imagination within this intricate and usually concrete structure of images. It is a highly evocative and stimulating kind of poetry, well suited to our study of abstracting essences with the body.

Let us examine some sample poems to see the kinds of patterns we can work from.

> *Tremble, burial mound—*
> *my lamenting voice—*
> *the autumn wind.*
> BASHŌ

Note how each line evokes its own image and action. As we shift from the image of a trembling mound to the voice in opposition, we are combining unlike entities (a trembling voice with ground that trembles); yet, in the desire to see the earth shake in sympathetic grief, we also see a poetic identity between voice and ground (mourner and the earth that holds the beloved dead). Then, we pivot on voice to wind, and we see a new association: the voice of grief is the voice of autumn, its cold and sad wind. Another interpretation (perhaps more accurate from the point of view of the poet) is to imagine the "trembling mound" is not earth, but a funeral pyre. In that case the trembling would be the actual physical trembling of the wood supporting the body just before its inward collapse. In this interpretation of the same poem the combined images imply the similarity of the crackling weakened burning wood to the mourning voice to the cold and bitter wind. Neither interpretation is necessarily correct—nor is "correct interpretation" important. But in either interpretation the density of the language is important. Thus, with the shifting perceptions we have a dramatic buildup to the final incorporation of all three images as a poetic whole.

> *The lightning flashes,*
> *zigzag—piercing the darkness*
> *a night-heron's scream.*
> BASHŌ

Again we have a second line pivot in the ambivalence: lightning pierces and so does the scream. Each image is succinct but vivid. We see lightning; we see and perhaps feel the piercing; and we hear the scream. Yet while the imagistic picture is specific and hard, it opens up into metaphorical suggestion well beyond the perception of a scene.

> *For I, who am leaving*
> *for you, who are staying*
> *two autumns for us.*
> BUSON

This poem implies a dramatic vignette. We contemplate the paradox that one season is divided by the parting of intimates.

I feel a piercing chill:
in the bedroom, my dead wife's comb
under my bare foot.

BUSON

Indeed, a whole scene of poignant drama is imagistically sketched in this poem with that final mundanely haunting climactic detail—he is stepping on the comb. The "hurt" is considerable. Consider the differences created by these two equally sound translations of the same haiku by Buson.

A	B
This morning's breezes	*See the morning winds*
I can see them rippling a	*how they are blowing the hair—*
caterpillar's hair.	*a caterpillar?*

Can you see how A is *scenic:* we see motion first, then rippling effects become visible, and then, as if a close-up camera withdraws from the scene we behold, very close, the fur of a caterpillar. All along we suspected it would be grass, and we are pleasantly surprised. But B depends more on *rhetoric*, that is, we hear the speaker's voice as he moves us to his surprising query, whose answer must be "yes."

For further haiku consult a good collection with translations in modern English. [*An Introduction to Haiku*, by Harold G. Henderson (New York: Anchor; 1958) is a useful collection.] You can even compose your own. Now that we have the medium, let us proceed to the "Haiku Exploration."

1. Get into groups of three to five. Select a haiku poem and analyze it for five or six minutes, deciding as a group how it works and what is essential in it.

2. When decided, begin as a group to prepare a version of its *physicalized essence*, by exploring physically as a group. Be sensitive to the *technique* of the poem, but do not try to illustrate it literally: Seek the *essence* of the images and its pattern of unfolding. Remember the qualities of surprise, for example, and the way the three lines build into a single effect.

3. Keep what works, throw away the rest, until your physicalization carries the same message as the poem. You should need no more than fifteen more minutes.

4. Then, for the presentation in class, the poem can be read before, after, or during the presentation (as in a Greek chorus).

5. A class discussion should follow the presentation of the essence, so that the problems encountered in the poem may be compared to the results.

A take-home assignment should carry the work over to the next meeting. Have each actor select his own haiku and prepare its essence for the next meeting. Presentation should be of the same order as for the groups.

ACTION VERB*

The purpose of this exploration is to help the actor gain easier access to the "action verb" activity by working on its physical essence. With a partner, set up a situation or work from a scene and prepare action verb capsulizations. Begin lying on the floor, close enough to one another to sense the other's presence. Attain a neutral state. Then let the situation and action verb soak in, until you have a strong inward sense of it. When ready, begin to move around, developing the feel of the action verb. When plugged into yourself, begin relating to the other and follow through with your action as long as you can. Generally, most situations and scenes demand a winner, one whose action verb defeats the other.

> VARIATION 1: When ready, move gradually from the physical abstraction into a realistic version of the imagined situation or the scene itself. Verbalizing is helpful, but if a scene is used, verbatim dialogue need not be essential.

> VARIATION 2: In the middle of a successful abstraction, the pair will be commanded to freeze. Then roles are reversed. If the interplay has been intense, each will be familiar enough with the other's action verb and physicalized identity to effect a smooth exchange. Then after this proceeds well, another freeze, and a return to the original role. Then after a while, a slow transition into a realistic vein with dialogue.

ENERGY

To restate an earlier theme, there are three primary elements essential to all movement—Space, Time, and Energy. Only space can be specifically measured by our five senses. Both Time and Energy are hypotheti-

---

*This is a movement study inspired from observing Archie Smith's graduate acting class at Penn State working on an improvisation in seizing the basic activity of a scene, and expressing a capsulized version of that activity in action verb units: to kill, to seduce, to surround, to flee, and so forth. More specifically the action verb can be effectively used to focus a line, a word, or even a pause, by conceiving that small unit in terms of specific and graphic physical gestures or actions you would like to use on a given character, but you use the word and/or body language to effect the socially acceptable variant. The actor may subverbally conceive an action verb then, in this manner: "With this (word, line, glance, stare, wink, shrug, pause, etc.) I (the character) am going to (kiss his cheek, kick her in the belly, stroke her face tenderly, shove a knife in him, slap him, tweak her nose, spit in her face, etc.)." In this case, the more specific the conceptualization of the physical action (the Action Verb), and the more organic the connection between visualization, and emotional justification, the better the tool. As long as the actor is working in Essence, and is trained to *not hurt another actor*, this is a powerful, useful tool.

cal and only dimly understood concepts that most branches of education do not even consider as relevant to their task. This is no less true of the study of theatre arts in general. But since it is one of the three primary elements essential to all movement, any serious study of stage movement must attempt to deal with these concepts. Time and space exist without us, but without energy we could not move, and so we would not exist at all.

Before I begin this portion of study, I always ask my classes this basic question: "When you think about energy what terms or images come to mind?" Typical answers are "solar power," "atomic power," "a lot," "the sun," "horsepower," and so on. Occasionally a student with a scientific orientation will say "Energy is the capacity to do work and overcome resistance." I have had no one, in all my classes, come forward with a practical definition that would be useful to a dance or theatre artist. Why should they? There is no generally accepted method of dealing with this phenomenon outside serious modern dance theorists and practitioners. Indeed, my understanding of the elements of energy come from my studies of Laban and modern dance as these studies were affected by my theatre studies, and it is this practical definition that I use in dealing with actors.

Briefly, we never see energy. All we ever see is the result of energy: We see the lightbulb turn on when we throw the switch; we see the water wheel turn as the water spills over the paddles, we see the trees bend in the wind, and the blades of the windmill turn; we see the airplane fly, the car speed away, and the horses as they strain for the finish line—but we never see the energy that causes these things to happen. Our eyes are not equipped for that. Let us then concentrate on that which we can see.

Energy Qualities

In all movement we can see evidence of six different types of application of energy. By the outward appearance of the movement, we can understand how the energy is being applied. With this visual evidence we can assign different qualitative definitions for each of the six different types and illustrate and validate each through human movement.

1. *Sustained or lyrical*—This is a constant even flow of energy, which produces movement identified by its smooth unchanging dynamic. Whether the person is moving fast or slow, no noticeable change occurs in the speed, rhythm, or effort needed to execute any movement in the phrase.

2. *Percussive*—Contrasted to "sustained," this is energy that strongly pulses, at regular or irregular intervals, to produce sudden and dynamic changes in the amount of effort needed, and in the speed and rhythm in which the movement is

executed. This causes sharp, sudden changes in the dynamics of the movement.

3. *Vibratory*—This is a kind of cross between "sustained" and "percussive" in that the energy is applied continually and dynamically changes direction and intensity at regular or irregular intervals, but at a speed and rhythm too fast to be either "sustained" or "percussive."

4. *Suspend*—This is sort of a hybrid type of "sustained" application of energy that produces a unique visual impression quite distinct from normal sustained movement. Here the energy is constantly and evenly applied so as to just barely combat the forces of gravity acting upon the body. It produces the visual image of a body rising slowly, or suspended at a height and altitude that is barely sufficient to hold it there.

5. *Collapse*—The exact opposite of "suspend," these two qualities are almost inseparable in human movement. One cannot "suspend" indefinitely; eventually one must release or discontinue expending energy, and when that happens the body "collapses." This may be done slowly ("sustained") or quickly ("percussive"), but the end result is the same: The body falls back in on itself and down toward the ground as gravity takes over.

6. *Swinging*—This is a particular kind of dynamic interaction of "suspend"/"collapse," and "percussive"/"sustained." Energy is "percussively" applied at the beginning of the movement phrase, and the body "collapses" progressively in a "sustained" manner until it rebounds up into a "suspended" quality as gravity in a gradual ("sustained") manner takes over once again. Then the next movement phrase begins again with another "percussive" surge of energy.

In our everyday experiences we can find each Energy quality employed in the movement of the people we encounter. Certain mental and physical states tend to produce the same Energy quality in people's movement regardless of race, language, sex, or beliefs. Anger tends to produce percussive movement. Cold, fear, or intense anxiety tend to produce vibratory movement. A person trying to make a decision, or trying to hear urgent sounding cries for help almost invariably suspends his body and holds very still so that the senses and mind can most efficiently function. Gaiety, especially in small children, leads people into a swinging carefree bodily carriage. Formal occasions requiring solemnity seem to dictate sustained movement in most individuals, whereas despair, gloom, and defeat seem to leave people collapsed in on themselves and slumped on furniture carelessly. Even certain combinations of qualities can be predicted if the physical state is known. Observe a person in an extreme state of intoxication and you should be able to note a very clear combination of suspend and collapse qualities operating as he or she struggles to remain erect—and even to appear sober.

Of course, there are exceptions to these generalities, and there are many other kinds of mental and physical states that can produce each of the examples offered, but we are not in the business of cataloguing here. The business of theatre artists consists partially of making accurate and meaningful observations in the world inside and around us. These concepts of Energy qualities are one of the most useful tools I have found to aid in this process of "seeing."

All that remains for the stage movement teacher, actor, and director is to find a way to make this new tool work for them. That is what this period of study is designed to permit. The way to proceed is to place the preliminary observations on the individual.

Every person tends to have his distinctive energy pattern, with perhaps a single dominating quality and one or two complementary qualities. So an untrained actor with a percussive primary quality may have difficulty basing his actions on a swinging or sustained quality. Exploring all the ways energy is released should give an actor a greater range of energy choices, provide him with a more supple body, and thus increase his range of character choices. (A public figure or entertainer can develop or cultivate a movement personality, stressing one of these energy qualities. Don Knotts did so with the vibratory quality, Bob Hope with a swinging one. A parlor game is inherent in this material: Is Dean Martin's performing image based on a "sustained" energy quality? Richard Nixon's gestural style "percussive"?)

While an actor may become President, one-dimensional movie star, or nightclub entertainer, it is ever the desire that as a serious actor he will attempt to do more than drag the self-same mannerisms complete with his immediately recognizable energy quality into every role he attempts on the stage or screen.

Energy Transformations

The warmups for this unit can be tailored to reinforce the concept of the six Energy Qualities: note for the class how the plié or knee-bend is done with sustained, even quality, and the four-count stretch with a percussive one. But to enhance the effect of this reinforcement, one can tinker with the exercises in unaccustomed qualities, so the four-count stretch might be done in a sustained or swinging manner. As has been said before, one should try to invent and adapt exercises to suit Exploration topics to be covered, and Exploration topics to suit class talent, attention, and capabilities—so that you use previous lessons to help teach and focus the next or future topics.

General Improvisation: (Short Form)

This is the introduction to Energy that each class receives. Before any warmup, with no prior discussion, I inform the class that the next period of study is to be Energy. I then ask the question: "When you think of energy, what terms or images come to mind?" All responses are valuable. After all, these are the things they think of when the term is mentioned. Many students are at a loss to say anything. This is neither unusual nor unexpected, because most people just have not thought about energy in any real depth.

Once the students have said all that they can on the subject, I explain that all movement occurs as a result of certain applications of energy on matter and that in this class we will analyze energy in terms of the movement qualities that the various applications of energy we as human beings employ to effect movement.

This General Improvisation will be repeated at the end of the warmup to reinforce the nature of the six energy qualities. The difference is that more time will be spent on each quality because we do not want the students to do any really strenuous movement before they are warmed up. So this initial exploration for each quality should be no more than thirty seconds, just enough to acquaint the students loosely with each one, while limiting the risk factor. After the warmup several minutes of exploring each quality in the same general manner will provide the student with a less superficial understanding of the subject.

SUSTAINED OR LYRICAL

1. This is a smooth even flow of energy that results in a similarly smooth even flow of the body.
2. Try moving your arm in a sustained or lyrical manner. Notice there are no sudden changes in direction or dynamic.
3. Move other parts of your body in this quality. Explore the range of movements you can use with your head, to torso, legs, hands and still maintain the lyrical quality.
4. Now explore with the whole body. Do not feel tied to one spot on the floor. Don't stay small and tentative in your movements.
5. Don't make all your movements slow as in a dream; speed them up as fast as you can and still keep the movement sustained—free of jerks and stops.
6. Let yourself go. Trust your body.
7. Good. Now let's move to a quality opposite this one in feeling tone.

PERCUSSIVE

1. This is just what the name implies: dynamic, powerful changes in the application of energy that causes sudden, abrupt, or jerky movements.
2. Explore the use of percussive movements with your body. Really let go of this movement.
3. That's enough of percussive.

VIBRATORY

1. If you move in a long series of very short, jerky percussive movements, a vibratory quality is produced.
2. Try vibrating just your hand; your head; your leg. Now your whole body.
3. This takes a lot of energy to maintain for any great length of time.
4. That's enough. So far we have tried sustained, percussive, and vibratory qualities.

SUSPEND AND COLLAPSE

1. The next two qualities operate together. They are suspend (I suspend my arm) and collapse (I let my arm fall to my side.)
2. Try to suspend just your arm. Hold it there. Eventually it must collapse down. Let the energy go.
3. Explore suspend and collapse in various parts of your body. Suspend just a finger, then let it collapse. Just your hand, your head, your upper body. Explore easily.
4. Good. This is the normal interaction of suspend and collapse. Let's move into the last application of energy on the body, which is another type of suspend/collapse.

SWINGING

1. Swinging starts in suspend, and with just a slightly percussive motion proceeds to a collapse and rebounds up to suspend. Then the cycle starts again.
2. Swing your arm. Explore swinging in various parts of your

body. Isolate the quality in your head, leg, and your upper torso.

3. Now, we will go into the warmup, paying attention to these various energy qualities as we use them in our exercises.

Discussion of the six qualities does not occur until the end of this first class. The introduction I prepared for this book is unnecessary and undesirable for an actual movement class. Once this initial movement exploration has been coupled with the ensuing warmup and the following in-depth exploration, students will have a much more immediate understanding of energy than any amount of discussion would provide.

At the end of the warmup during this introductory class, the three frustration jumps should be performed in any three energy qualities the individual student chooses to employ. From their position of total collapse at the end of the three jumps, I then move once again into the General Improvisation, but this time students will explore each in depth.

GENERAL IMPROVISATION (IN DEPTH)

1. Bring yourself to a neutral state. Allow your breathing to return to normal, release all tension, relax into yourself, and clear your mind.
2. Once your breathing has returned to normal, rise, in a sustained application of energy, into your natural alignment, and check your alignment by pressing up through your feet.
3. Now begin exploring a sustained application of energy.
    a. Isolate movements in your hands, then incorporate your arms.
    b. Isolate the movement in your legs, your head; then just your torso.
    c. Now involve the whole body. Don't allow yourself to stay rooted to the same spot. Let the movement use various ranges, levels, and directions in space. Use the entire space in your exploration.
    d. Don't make all the movement slow and dreamlike. You can move fairly fast and still keep the movement in a sustained energy quality. See how fast you can move and still be sustained in your movement. What kind of movements do you have to use to do this?
    e. Now explore sustained movement in any way you wish. Pay attention to how this affects you internally.
4. Let's move to percussive.
    a. Try exploring freely in the percussive energy quality.
    b. Take the time to explore it in a variety of different ways. Don't be satisfied with one way of moving percussively.
    c. Does this affect you differently than did moving in a sustained

manner? Let the way this movement affects you guide your exploration. Keep the movements abstract. Just let the essences of your emotion dictate your movements.

    d. All right, now release that emotion, shake out your tension, and let's move on to the next energy quality.

5. Vibratory.
    a. Try vibrating various body parts—hand, arm, foot, head, and so on.
    b. Take the vibration into your whole body.
    c. What kind of feelings does this elicit?
    d. Explore vibratory any way you wish to, and allow your feeling again guide your exploration.
    e. Relax. Vibratory uses much more energy than the other qualities, so it is difficult to sustain for long periods.

6. Now let's move to suspend and collapse.
    a. Start exploring suspend and collapse with just a finger. Lift it up, and let is collapse back to place.
    b. Add on other fingers until you have the whole hand suspending and collapsing.
    c. Slowly add on body parts suspending higher and collapsing lower until you collapse onto the ground.
    d. Explore this now freely and see if it will elicit some sort of feeling tone in you, then let that feeling change and guide your exploration.
    e. Release that feeling, shake out your body; let's go to the last energy quality.

7. Swinging.
    a. Try swinging your arm. Add on the other arm, let the torso swing with them. Finally, the head joins in.
    b. See if you can keep the sense of the swing as you move around the room. How can you move across the floor to the other side of the room and keep the feel of the swing? Try different ways of moving in various directions and still maintain a swinging quality.
    c. Explore it any way you want to. Let the body take over.
    d. See what kind of feeling tone this brings out of your body.
    e. Let the feeling help your exploration.
    f. Good. Now relax, shake out your body.

8. Summation.
    a. By now you should be able to see that the different energy qualities do affect you emotionally, especially when they are used as broadly as we have here.
    b. But the effect is still there on both subject and observer even when the movement is much more subtle.
    c. To prove this, the next exploration will be geared to revealing the truth of that statement.

ENERGY AND GESTURE

1. Everyone do some functional gesture—scratch your nose, or brush your hair out of your eyes, pull up your socks—anything that you do normally everyday.

2. Do it several more times trying to notice how you do it. What kind of energy is involved?

3. Are you performing it in a percussive, sustained, or vibratory manner?

4. Why? What other ways could this same gesture be done?

5. Try doing this same gesture in a vibratory manner. How does this change the way you feel while doing the gesture?

6. Now use percussive; lyrical; suspend and collapse; swinging. Do each several times while trying to sense the difference in your perception of the gesture.

7. Now do the gesture again the way you normally do it. Ask yourself now, "What is there in the performance of the gesture that is me? Why do I perform that gesture in that energy quality and not another?"

8. Take another gesture. This time a social gesture. And repeat the process (steps 2 to 7).

9. Notice the similarities and differences in the energy applications of your Functional and Social gestures. Can you identify the reasons for both the similarities and the differences? How? Why?

Depending on the length of class time and the capacity of the class members, "Energy and Gesture," as well as the next two explorations ("Walking/Energy," and "Internal/External Dependence") could be combined with the General Improvisations to provide an excellent introductory class for Energy. In many cases, however, these Explorations will have to be spread out over two class periods due to time restraints and student endurance levels.

WALKING/ENERGY

1. Walk around the room as you usually do. Note your use of energy.

2. Now make your walk take on a percussive quality.

3. Change to a swinging quality. Try several different ways of walking in a swinging quality. What different images come to mind?

4. Move into suspend and collapse. Note the changes, and the similarities if there are any.

5. Vibrate in your walk. You may have difficulty walking in a vibratory manner but try it different ways. It is possible.

6. Now sustained. A complete change in the feeling tone. Don't just move slowly. Try walking at different speeds and still maintain the sustained quality.

7. Now come back to your normal walk. Do you notice anything new about your use of energy?

Internal/External Dependence

Before launching directly into the next Exploration (as I would in an actual class), it is beneficial to note several observations about the relationship of the internal and external realities. As has been discussed earlier in this book, all actors do not work the same way. Even using the same tools no two actors will approach the project of revealing the secrets of any character in the same way. To restate a previous theme, there are only three basic approaches to characterization:

1. *External to Internal*—An actor can put on the mask, say the words, and try to discover what the external manifestations indicate he must be feeling to look the way he looks and say the things he's saying. Thus, the external informs the intellect which sculpts the internal reality.

2. *Internal to External*—He can build up such a wealth of emotion, compassion for, and understanding of the character (through the use of native empathy, sense-memory and other tools) that his inner reality radiates outward. So the internal reality defines the external appearance.

3. *External and Internal*—An actor can use one, then the other, or both at the same time, allowing both to affect each other.

In most cases (even though most novice actors do not realize it) actors tend to be extremely pragmatic, and hence use anything that works for them. That means that actors tend to approach roles both from the inside and from the outside. Oddly, many actors choose to believe totally in one method of working (*External to Internal* or *Internal to External*) so much so that they are blind to and feel incapable of working in the other manner.

This is a great problem because it inevitably makes an actor either unsure (because he realizes his crippling inability), or grossly overconfident (because he is blind to his lack of perspective). The interlocking mechanisms serve to provide for perspective, balance, and a fail-safe system that mutually benefits and reinforces decisions and their execution. Without this system any actor is at a great disadvantage.

There may be many reasons for this, but principle among possible explanations is the very pragmatic nature of actors. Because actors use what works, many actors who have found early success (not always the best gauge) using the mask approach scorn any other, and those who've learned to "spill their guts" disdain their so-called "empty technician" friend's approach. The thing that is so strange about this phenomenon is that most of the people who hold this attitude have either never tried "the other" approach, or did so with such a jaundiced eye that they poisoned their own sensitivity and so doomed the attempt, thus "proving" to themselves that the attempt was useless in the first place!

Although there may be no cure for these extreme cases of jaundice, the majority of student actors should find the following Exploration very illuminating and helpful. This is a rare opportunity because actors have very few situations in which the two approaches are so clearly delineated. Especially useful is the fact that the two approaches are attempted in the same narrow band of time under a single Exploration that is specifically designed to reveal the positive values of both approaches. Intellectually we may understand the relationship of form and content, but here students have the chance to discover in very immediate (emotional and physical) terms, some of that reality within themselves.

THE EXTERNAL TO INTERNAL APPROACH

1. Relax onto your backs. Breathe deeply. Clear your mind and body of all tension. Bring yourself to a neutral state.

2. Choose at random one of the energy qualities (if you choose suspend, you must do collapse also) and try to feel what it is like to move in this energy quality without actually moving.

3. Now begin to explore moving in this quality. Take your time and explore it fully.

4. Let it affect you emotionally. What kind of emotion or memory does this call to mind? Allow your movement to change as you discover an emotion that fits that quality.

5. Do not change the basic quality. If you are moving percussively, continue moving percussively, but let the percussive quality be textured by the emotional tone.

6. See if this problem or emotion will work itself out. Follow through with your exploration while you try to discover the natural conclusion to the emotion or situation. Let the quality change.

7. If you feel like relating to those around you in essence form, do so nonverbally, but if you do not wish to relate to others around you, you don't have to.

8. Allow the tension to drain from you. Relax onto the floor. Don't

just let it fall off. Follow through with your situation and its resolution. Take your time, but don't hold onto it. When it's over, it's over. Just relax. Breathe deeply. Clear yourself. Bring yourself back to a neutral state.

THE INTERNAL TO EXTERNAL APPROACH

1. In your relaxed state, search your mind for a situation or experience that caused you to have a strong or very definite emotional reaction. This could be a happy or sad, angry or joyous experience. It could be one that made you feel empty, confused, anxious, or hopeless; or it could be one that made you feel just the opposite. If you are depressed today, don't pick one that will aid your depression. That is the only restriction on the memory you can choose.

2. Fill yourself with the memory of this experience. Try to see the place and people; hear the sounds. Can you recall any smells or other textures of the experience? What caused the emotion? Try to feel the emotion that was caused by the episode you experienced.

3. Once you have a firm grasp of the situation and the emotion— once you have filled yourself with it, and are ready—allow your body to respond to the stimulus you are feeling. Let the situation or emotion suggest an energy quality to help your exploration of it.

4. Do not rush yourself. Take your time, and keep the movements free and abstract. See if your movement can help in your recollection of the event.

5. You can respond to people working near you if they aid in your exploration. See if there is someone who seems to fit into the recollection—an opponent, a friend, a lover, Mother, Father.

6. See if you can find a resolution to the situation. Follow through with the exploration. Don't impose an artificial resolution. Let it work itself out.

7. When you have gone through either to resolution or realization of stalemate, let yourself slowly release the situation, allow the tension to drain from you, and collapse gradually back onto the floor.

8. Breathe deeply, clear yourself. Come back to a neutral state. Relax.

If this exploration ends the class, the discussion will probably center on the question of which method worked better for each individual and why. It is important to point out that neither one is *the* way of working, both are acceptable. If one works inside to outside, the exterior manifestation of the internal reality is as important as the ability to conjure the internal reality. And if one works outside to inside, the outside is only a shell. Without the inner reality to fill it, the performance, the character, the actor is hollow. Either fault is really only the age-old problem of "sound and fury signifying nothing."

Energy Combinations

Occasionally an actor will be confronted with a character whose major obstacle is himself. The character must conquer fear or must try to appear calm although he is quite agitated, or perhaps has conflicting desires about the presence and actions of an aggressive member of the opposite sex. The problem of how to physicalize and make this visible to the audience in a realistic or believable manner is sometimes impossible to solve for untrained actors.

This exploration is designed to provide one possible tool for dealing with this problem. Aside from that, however, it is a challenging and creative tool to help cement the comparisons and contrasts of energy qualities and demonstrates the need for disciplined concentration in the acting craft.

EXTERNAL TO INTERNAL

1. Relax onto the floor and clear yourself. Breathe deeply and release all tension.

2. Select two contrasting energy qualities at random. Stay relaxed.

3. You are going to try to perform both of these energy qualities simultaneously. To do this you may have to put one energy quality in one part of your body (say the right side, or from just your hips down) and the other quality in another part.

4. When you think you have found the proper body parts for the energy qualities, begin to move around in these contrasting qualities.

5. See if one will take over dominance. See if there is a resolution to the problem of the two qualities working simultaneously.

6. Is there an emotional state created by this problem? See if this can be resolved in any way.

7. Follow through with your exploration until there is resolution or stalemate and then gradually release the tension and the problem and come back to a neutral state.

1. Now recall a situation in which you experienced conflicting desires or emotions.

2. Fill yourself with the situation, and when you are in touch with the emotions it created, begin to explore the situation physically.

3. See if one emotion can cause one type of energy quality and the other a contrasting energy quality. (Suspend and collapse are two separate qualities for this Exploration.)

4. See if you can find a resolution of your problem.

5. Does one emotion and energy quality win out or suppress the other?

6. Follow through with your exploration until there is a resolution or stalemate, then gradually release the tension, situation, and emotion and relax back onto the floor.

7. Clear yourself. Breathe deeply. Relax. Bring yourself back to a neutral state.

Self-Discovery: An Energy Essence Study (A Take-Home Assignment)

This is a study of one's own characteristic energy quality. We all have a dominating energy quality, a product of our psychology and unique socialization experiences. Usually, in fact, individuals primarily employ some dynamic blend of two primary energy qualities. Rather than a single energy quality, most people tend to use a combination of the "me I want to be perceived as being" quality (that is, perhaps, a sustained, cool, methodical, and emotionally controlled persona) that is just as much a part of their natural energy quality as the "me that I want to keep people from seeing" quality (that may be a percussive, driving force of ambition and perfection). The two qualities, whatever they are, work together, not usually in the manner of Jekyll and Hyde (where one dominates for four hours, and then the other takes control), but in a more subtle, effective, and efficient way depending on the nature of our changing reality.

From the information learned in the previous Explorations and from the knowledge you have gleaned from the long years of living with yourself, prepare an abstraction of your own basic movement quality, a brief, perhaps half-minute study that reveals your employment of your one or two primary applications of energy in a typical day, both the essence and the realistic manner—how you walk, sit down, put on your coat, and so on.

The session should end with a discussion period and students should critique and compare notes on how accurate or revealing the studies were.

We will return to Energy in the Applications (Chapter 5).

PHYSICAL ESSENSE OF SELF

As a Take-Home Assignment there is a very difficult exploration designed to complete the earlier self-awareness process by forcing the actor to come to an abstraction of his physical being.

Prepare a short movement study in which you deal with your pronounced movement mannerisms, the defects and the virtues. This is purely an external exercise focused on how you move, not the psychological motivations for the movement. Do an abstraction of these mannerisms and prepare a parallel realistic synopsis. Then in class you will do both in a half-minute or so presentation. Do not get emotionally worked up in this process. Relax and enjoy your movement portrait. Enjoy the discussion, too; it should be very illuminating.

TIME

Of the three primary elements of movement (space, time, and energy) time is perhaps the most difficult to deal with in stage movement. Time is conceptually more difficult than the other two elements because while you can see and feel space, and you can see the effects of the application of energy, time is neither tactile, nor is it, in most cases, as easily controllable. In fact, time is the most intractable concept man possesses simply because it is so damned subjective. One person's estimate and perception of the passage of time is so radically different from another's that without modern timepieces there could be no agreement about the "amount" of time that it takes to read from the start of this paragraph to the end. Do you know how long it took you?

Knowing that our sense of time is almost entirely subjective, however, is the key to unlocking the secrets we as theatre artists need to reveal. What we are looking for, then, is not the precise measurement or quantitative analysis of time that our scientists so desperately search for; no, what we need are tools to understand how our perceptions of time are effected.

Fortunately there are many things that we already know about our perceptions of time. For instance, we know that when we are bored and have nothing to do a minute can seem like an hour. We know that when we are late for an appointment and are stopped at a red light, that same minute can seem like an eternity. When trying to write a paper that was due last week, the minute spent agonizing over the choice of words, or looking up the spelling can flash by without our notice. Rushing to catch a plane leaves us wondering why our watch suddenly speeded up.

We all know, in short, that our sense of time changes with our emotional states and the situations that cause them. Oddly, most of us tend to forget time is more complicated than our watches, bus schedules, and calendars lead us to believe. One minute is not the same as the next; one day is totally different than the one before; and one year in the life of a three year old is altogether different than the same year for an octogenarian.

Even within the same event there are contrasting perceptions of time. In the first year of Ronald Reagan's presidency, as he was walking jauntily out of a Washington hotel with his entourage, a would-be assassin stepped from the crowd and emptied his revolver at the President. It is obvious that the assassin's time sense was dramatically different from that of President Reagan, the newsmen, his entourage, and the casual onlookers clustered a few feet away. Once the first shot was fired, however, the "Sunday morning stroll" atmosphere rapidly vanished and time condensed. Before the shots there was "all the time in the world" to do what everyone needed to do, then in less time than it takes to think the word "assassin," there was not enough time to do anything—to duck, to dodge, to evacuate the President, to stop the attacker. The film and videotape revealed all this in minute and gruesomely graphic detail, revealing even the cameraman's wince. Each person perceived and reacted to the threat in his own way at different times.

So how do we deal with time in a stage movement class? What terms do we use, and how can we manipulate our sense of time to further develop our understandings of its many facets? Thankfully, there is at least one group of artists who out of necessity have spent centuries dealing with the problem of time, and it is in this direction that we, as theatre artists, must turn.

Musicians have, probably since the dawn of mankind, been involved in the process of defining and manipulating the various elements that control our perception of time. The theoretical basis is so firm by now that both dance and theatre artists can, and to varying degrees do effectively, use at least the basic principles of music theory.

There are five basic principles I use in explorations of time. Although the theory comes primarily from music, the application of that theory can be expressed in terms of movement. And although the description of the phenomenon may seem at first purely external, keep in mind that, as with all elements of movement, it in reality is merely another way of describing the external manifestation of some internal phenomenon.

Five Basic Principles of Time

1. *Duration*—How long it takes to complete a movement, or set of movements.

2. *Tempo*—How fast a movement or movement phrase is completed; speed.

3. *Rhythmic pattern*—The regulation of tempo and duration of movements into ordered sets.

4. *Accent*—The emphasis within the rhythmic pattern of movements. The strongest and most significant movements in a movement phrase.

5. *Counterpoint*—Two or more contrasting sets of time elements existing simultaneously either within one person's movement, or between two or more people (that is, one person sitting languidly back on a chair with his foot rapidly tapping the floor; one person moving slowly, another quickly, and so on).

While these definitions seem fairly simple, confusion sometimes occurs when students try to ponder the difference between Duration and Tempo. Partly this is so because they are in some sense similar because they can be used to describe the same event. They are dramatically different, however, because tempo is concerned with speed (how fast the car was going) while duration is concerned with length of time (how long it took the car to get there). Accent can be a tricky concept to explain, but it becomes much simpler by demonstrating. Have students clap their hands four times keeping the sound at a constant level (note the lack of accent), and then have them clap their hands four times trying to make the sound loudest on the last clap (note the accent or stress placed on the last clap). The last clap, then, is one example of a movement that is similar to other movements, but different because it used more energy and larger swings of the hands and produced a noticeably louder sound. You could note that even without the sound, the movement would still be noticeably different from the others and so is still accented.

Once students have noticed that, you can have them move forward around the room in a walk, placing emphasis on, say, the first step out of each four, so that they are stepping emphatically *one*, two, three, four, *one*, two, three, four, and so on. Then you could have them try the same pattern, or another accented pattern, in other parts of the body (say, one, *two*, three, *four*). These three definitions are fairly easy to communicate even to the uninitiated student.

Before moving on to the major problem of defining Rhythmic Patterns, let's acknowledge and further develop another musical concept that has just been introduced. By placing four regular pulses of movement of the same duration in a sequence we have created a time pattern called a measure. Specifically, the pattern established above is

¼ time (simply four beats to a measure). This is so frequently used in music that it is called common time. Emphasis or Accent can occur on any of the four beats, and it is still ¼ or common time. There are many other measures or time signatures that are used: 2/4 (two beats to a measure), ¾ (three beats to a measure), 6/8 (six beats to a measure), 5/4 (five beats to a measure), and others. But the basic principles apply to each. By placing a limit on the number of beats you will consider as a unit, and then repeating the unit, you provide yourself with a frame of reference—a measure—by which you compare and compose the elements.

Now, to eliminate another possible problem that *may* develop, let's state here that there is a fairly broad spectrum of speed (tempo) at which these accented or unaccented patterns may be played, and still remain essentially the same structurally (that is, the same relative measure of time). Watch what happens to the feeling tone, however, when the speed or tempo is increased. While each beat remains the same Duration relative to the next within a given measure, the faster the tempo, the shorter the Duration of each beat and measure. Take the "Plains Indian Cliche" (*one*, two, three, four) from a very slow tempo gradually to a very fast tempo, and it turns into a speeding steam locomotive. It is still ¼ time—the accent remains the same (so does the Rhythmic Pattern)—but the internal feeling evoked is totally altered, along with the movement quality of improvising students.

Now, to change the rhythmic pattern within the ¼ time frame, we must add one further consideration: Let's change the duration of one or more of the counts or numbers within the measure. Take the unaccented pattern "one, two, three, four" and elongate the first count so that it is exactly as long in duration as the first two counts (one and two) combined. The pattern thus produced would be: one, three, four, one, three, four, and so on. Count two is counted (there are still four beats to the measure); it is merely hidden, or included in a longer count use. Another way to alter the duration of the numbers is to shorten the duration of one or more numbers by one-half so that count one, for instance, has two equal pulses in the same duration as it would normally take to count one. The new rhythmic pattern thus produced would be: one, and, two, three, four, one, and, two, three, four, and so on.

Frequently used rhythmic patterns using this system are: one, and, two, and, three, and four, and; one, two, and, three, and, four; one, and, two, three, four, and; one, two, and, three, four, and. Notice none of these is accented, and accent, as we've noticed before, can completely alter the feeling tone of the music or movement thus affected. Also accent can be placed on any number or any corresponding "and" (that is, on or between any counted beat). For instance: "one, two, and, three, and four" can become "one, two, *and,* three, *and,* four" or "*one,* two, and, *three,* and, four." Notice, however, that while accent does affect feeling tone, the rhythmic pattern remains the same.

The last way to alter rhythmic pattern is by simply not playing a beat—by resting during that interval—so that there is a gap between numbers: one, (hold), three, four, one, (hold), three, four, etc.; or: one, (hold), and, three, four, one, (hold), and, three, four, etc.; or with accent: one, *and*, (hold), and, *three, four,* one, *and,* (hold), and, *three, four,* etc.

It must be noted that the rhythmic pattern in music is not the measure of the notes of what would normally be called the melody or harmony lines—it is rather the underlying structure of the music, the major pulse rate of the sound. Melody and harmony lines often incorporate either fewer or many more notes than exist in the rhythmic pattern, but both are inexorably focused, directed, and propelled by the basic rhythmic pattern. So it is with movement. While every single heartbeat, breath, and eye blink may not occur simultaneously with the pulses of the rhythmic pattern, the basic kinetic orientation is aligned with it naturally and spontaneously as the mind/body connection functions in an interactive state too fast for the conscious mind to calculate or control.

Rhythmic pattern changes for two reasons only—when the time signature changes and when the established pattern of beats within a single time signature changes.

To sum up all that has been said so far in terms I try to convey to my students: Each of the five elements defined alter our perception of time, whether or not we understand the definition of any of them. Understanding them intellectually and kinetically, however, gives you more understanding and control of your perception of time. If the effort to understand intellectually begins to interfere with the ability to understand kinetically—stop thinking, and just feel. This is rudimentary music theory that may, nonetheless, prove to be difficult conceptually, but it is practically universally simple to respond to.

Obviously students who have studied at least rudimentary music theory will be, initially at least, much more prepared to explore time in depth than students who have not and struggle to comprehend the concepts involved. The concepts I use in a stage movement class are really quite simple, but a student with no prior exposure to them tends to suffer from the effects of too much intellectual effort and too little spontaneity.

The key to teaching this section is to endeavor to bring in an element of lightness so that the class relaxes into their own natural sense of rhythm which in most cases is considerable, and for the few who have no sense of rhythm no amount of browbeating will help them grow in this capacity.

The following sequence of explorations are suggestions for approaching the subject of time and are meant partly to inspire other adaptations of the theory more lucidly explained in other texts. Keep in mind that for a movement class for actors the number of time signatures involved is quite finite (usually $\frac{2}{2}$, $\frac{2}{4}$, $\frac{3}{4}$, $\frac{4}{4}$, $\frac{5}{4}$, $\frac{6}{8}$ will be adequate).

The reason for this is that as bipedal creatures, we do not have occasion to use other more complicated theoretical structures to describe movement that occurs naturally in our day-to-day activities. Everyone moves in his own time pattern, whether regular or erratic, fast or lethargic. For example, we can often identify someone by his approach, his distinctive sound pattern in walking. But it is important for the actor to try out what it feels like to move in many time patterns that are not his own. The warmup for "time explorations" should again be geared to focusing on the time elements in the exercises so that the actor can anticipate the more difficult work later in the day.

DURATION (HOW LONG IT TAKES
TO COMPLETE A MOVEMENT)

1. Take a simple movement or gesture (opening and closing a door) and explore it with different durations. Then try other gestures.
2. Try walking, jumping, running, at different durations. The time it takes to move those three steps doesn't increase the number of steps.
3. Walk, stop, and freeze. Sense the duration of each. Move and freeze. Vary the duration of each. Feel the differences. This is an ambiguous set of directions, but you will know when you are feeling the sense of different durations.

TEMPO (SPEED—HOW FAST A MOVEMENT
OR MOVEMENT PHRASE IS COMPLETED)

1. Use a walk to improvise freely various tempos.
2. Perform a simple movement so fast your eyes can hardly follow it. Now repeat as slowly as you can manage it. Then try it with an in-between tempo. Try other movements and repeat three speeds.
3. By yourself, improvise changing tempos abruptly. Effect a sudden transition from a dream-like gliding into a Charley Chaplin walk, for example. Then work with three speed transitions, again abrupt and sudden, but with an intermediate buffer.

RHYTHMIC PATTERN (REGULATING TEMPO
AND DURATION INTO ORDERED SETS)

1. Improvise rhythmic patterns with several parts of the body. (*Examples:* Take a 4/4 meter [the rhythmic pattern being 1, 2, and 3, and 4] and explore the head or the torso. Or try 6/8 or 3/4 and build combinations [head to torso to leg to arm, etc.] changing part on each count.)

2. Now explore these rhythms, walking in different beats, or try a combination of walking, skipping, and running.

3. Take an everyday action, such as washing your hands, and explore it until you find its rhythmic pattern. Then alter that pattern.

CONVERSATION WITH RHYTHMIC PATTERN

1. Find a partner. You are going to communicate by use of rhythmic patterns. Use your whole body. Don't merely indicate. Think of and borrow from speech rhythms that fit certain emotions. Try anger, for instance, in a 1 and 2 and 3 and 4, at a fast tempo, with percussive movements.

2. This is an abstract conversation. When you think you are in tune with your partner, grade into a realistic conversation. Follow through to the end.

ACCENT

Just as the strongest stress in the intonation pattern of an utterance, accent in a movement phrase organizes and focuses the whole communication.

1. Since most accents are placed on the first beat in plain movement, it is important that you vary the accent pattern in the warmup for this day's work. Try one exercise with different accents: the pelvis rotation, say, with the accents moving from 2, 4, and 6, each rotation having a different accent.

2. Then make up a simple movement pattern across the floor several times with different accents each time.

3. By yourself, explore in a free improvisation all kinds of movements and accents. For example, take an everyday movement, such as putting on your coat, and play with the accent in the movement phrase.

4. Take a piece of dialogue and play with moving the accent in both the speech and the accompanying movement. Work on dialogue and gesture as one. Usually physical accents occur with verbal stress.

COUNTERPOINT OR CONFLICT

1. In a neutral state, standing, begin to explore the conflict possible in a simple external manipulation of the body. Oppose the right hand's slow, sustained quality while the left leg moves

sharply. Add more combinations with conflict. Now work the upper torso against the lower body. Then return to a neutral state. Think of cutting the body in half vertically, left and right; make one side graceful, lovely, and elegant, with lyrical movement; the other side is mean, hard, vicious, assertive, and perhaps percussive. Set up an opposition in the personalized states somehow, as long as there is a clash of movement qualities and feelings, between left and right. Fight. The two aspects must clash, as you move around. Maintain a close concentration or you will lose the clean opposition. Continue until one side triumphs. Then hold this quality. (This is a Grotowski-influenced exploration.) Relax. Release all tension. Breathe deeply, clear yourself.

2. Now as you lie on your back, relaxed and free from tension, try to remember a situation in which you had an internal conflict. Perhaps it was something you wanted to do as a child, but were afraid of doing. Maybe it was having to make a decision between two equally pleasant options; or two equally unpleasant options. Pick one situation you have experienced, and fill yourself with it. Without moving, try to feel the conflict within you as your desires, fears, and apprehensions do battle within you. Once you can feel the tension so strongly you can no longer remain still, allow your body to move with the tension. Try to let the inner tension express itself in its essence through your movement. You can react to those around you or not as you feel, but maintain the tension until you either find a resolution to the situation or the tension or both.

3. Get into pairs. You are going to explore the sense of counterpoint in pure movement (that is, movement that has no specific verbal dialogue inherent to its intent) with each other, responding to one another's movements. You answer each other with opposing or counterpointed moves and patterns.

4. Still in pairs, set up a situation of conflict within a specified personal relationship (this time the movement will imply inner states such as anger, impatience, love, and so forth). Begin by getting into a neutral state at a distance removed but near your partner. Think about the situation until you begin to comprehend it inwardly. Then get up and move about with one another. First to the essence of the conflict. Then, when ready, gradually move from the abstraction into the realistic improvisation implied by the continuing abstraction.

Because the improvisation occurs first using time as the focal point, and then moves to an internalized process, the analysis or revelation from the first part should reveal how external manipulations effect internal reactions, while the second part should reveal how the perceptions and use of time is effected by internal states. This exploration is especially helpful when you are going for the inner nature of a scene in class or in rehearsal.

A Music Exploration: A Summary

This is an improvisation to music aimed at incorporating all the elements of time you have been exploring. It works best using a prerecorded tape that has a wide range of music snippets—from electronic, pop, rock, classical, primitive, jazz, and country (see the example in Chapter 6, Practical Applications).

1. Move along in time with the rhythm, whatever it is, breaking or transforming it. You may place accents against the natural accents inherent in the music you are moving to.
2. Then work against the music, against the rhythm. If it is a percussive ¼ rhythm, move into a swinging gentle ¾, for example.
3. You may concentrate on the tempo, fast music and slow movement, and so on, as you move.
4. Then you can work with rhythmic patterns, seeing what types of things you feel when you try to do exactly the same rhythm that is being played.
5. Allow yourself to work alone or with others, either in counterpoint or in harmony. Do not feel inhibited by the orientation of the exploration; just respond freely to the stimulus that is around you.

Essential Rhythmic Patterns (A Take-Home Assignment)

Prepare a movement study on the essence of your own rhythmic pattern. Then add a realistic version. Go back to basic movements to find it—walking, drinking, lying down. Recall your energy study for some help.

Presentation should start with the abstraction. Then, when the abstraction is completed, perform your set of realistic movements. Then repeat the abstraction.

EMOTION

Emotion is perhaps the most direct avenue of approach to characterization. It is certainly an inevitable step in the preparation of any characterization. But it is also the most obvious of all the possible problems an actor can consider, and because it is such an important and obvious problem, many actors never get beyond it. And because they never get beyond the question "What is my character feeling?", the answers they find are quite likely to be largely arbitrary.

This is one reason why emotion is one of the last major areas I explore in my stage movement classes. To be sure, there are other considerations, chief among these being the concept I have used to guide the development of this system, that is, the progressive acquisition of skills. Since this is a movement class it was important first to develop each individual's ability to actualize through movement the various concepts he unconsciously employs in developing characterization. By illuminating the darkened areas of the students' perception of these essential elements before exploring emotion, they stand out in stark relief, and the student responds spontaneously to them. Rather than to worry how or even if these things affect him emotionally, his emotions become part of his perception, as is natural.

Since every element previously explored has had an emotional reaction tied to it, the actor should be more aware of the range and subtlety of the emotional response than he would be if the first day of class I said "Let's explore emotion." Now when we explore this most obvious area of characterization, the actor should have more information to draw from and be better prepared to use it effectively.

Lastly, by placing emotion near the end of this period of study, you place early and continuous emphasis on the fact that *acting is doing.* So many actors believe that all they must do is to feel. But it is important for them to understand that emotion is only a part of awareness—an organic response to stimuli that provides part of the motivation for our actions. It is only through our perceived actions that others (especially audiences) can understand either our emotions or motivations. Just feeling is not enough.

Once an actor understands and is in command of the other primary elements of stage movement, however, this last very important area of awareness will be an invaluable aid in completing the organic connection of mind and body. The final pieces of the puzzle should come tumbling quickly into place with very little intellectual effort.

FEELING-FORM-FLOW EXPLORATION

1. Get into a neutral state, mind cleared, tension drained, lying on the floor.
2. An emotion is suggested (joy, sorrow, love, hate). Develop the feeling of that emotion from some memories that make it your own.
3. When that emotion has absorbed your mind, get up and move about in the manner it seems to dictate.
4. Let your whole body respond to the emotion. Heighten the

feeling by expressing it throughout your body. Laugh or weep or cringe with the whole body.

5. Then localize the expressing, just with the foot or the hands, laughing, raging, or caressing.

6. Once the emotion exploration has run its course, a class discussion will help sort out the individual and collective experience. An important topic to cover is the comparison of this emotional manifestation with a purely external one.

FORM-FEELING-ELICITATIONS

1. Work into a deeply relaxed neutral state, mind completely cleared, and assume a standing position.

2. The instructor will call out a series of emotional states (utter desolation, cold loneliness, inner warmth and security, and so on) and you will respond instantaneously, on the spot striking a shape, position, or movement that that feeling provokes in you. Be as sensitive to the named emotion as possible (even though the rationale may strike you as callous) and respond as if the emotion were slapping you in the face, shocking you into its command.

3. Hold your response, but don't freeze. Move gently and slowly, keeping the emotional contours intact.

4. Meanwhile, reach inward to deepen the sense of the emotion. Let the form you are in seep into your core and touch your most sensitive responses. Perhaps personal images, remarks, memories will stir to life.

5. Move on in similar fashion with each of the emotions called out.

6. End the exploration with a discussion period.

MUSICAL CUES

1. Lie on the floor, in a neutral state, cleared and drained, with the lights dimmed.

2. The activity of this exploration is your reacting to musical cues, responding to the implied feeling or emotions, absorbing it, and then, letting your feelings flow out into your physical gesture and movement. (The tape may be of one rich and provocative composition or a medley of interesting pieces). Individuals respond variously to the same music, of course. Try only for the essence of the emotion. This is a free improvisation. You can work best by yourself. If some group interplay arises, you need not fight it.

From the frequent use of the "musical cues" approach you can see my reliance on this exploration technique. This is because I have found music to be of great assistance in freeing actors' imaginations and bodies; so that with the proper focus, the music allows the actors to teach themselves through an enjoyable, creative, and yet disciplined activity where they are free to come to their own understandings in their own way. This is the ultimate exploration technique, which can only be used after the early conditioning in body and mind. It is not unusual for students to request more frequent sessions in this activity. It is important, however, not to indulge this request too often because it tends to allow the student to rely too heavily on this tool.

There are more important uses for the lessons he has learned than to allow the actor to content himself in the revelry of a good "music cues" tape. After all, these lessons were intended to help him in his specific acting projects, and it is necessary for the total permanent acquisition of these lessons that the actor begin applying his new-found knowledge when he is ready.

The best time to begin applications is after actors have attained a relatively firm understanding of the basic elements of Space, Time, and Energy and have a firm grasp of the value and possibilities inherent in the Essence work. Use of these basic tools are essential to his or her continued development, not to mention continued interest. Somewhere along the line students are bound to ask themselves "Fascinating, but what good is it? How can this help me in my acting?".

The answer is that these are tools that will eventually aid them in unlocking the secrets or mysteries held within the words playwrites provide. From these words actors must find the information necessary to bring the people speaking them to life. Whether the words provided are few or many, unlocking the secrets from them is not often easy. There are many systems the actor can use, but few proceed from a physical base—or even an organic base. Now these actors have one, and in the next chapter I'll demonstrate how it works.

5
APPLICATIONS

I may as well begin with a note of despair, and then get on with the work. Certainly, there is no clear, straight, thoughtfully marked trail up the mountain to successful characterization. About brilliant inspired acting there is always that ineffable air. Audience, director, and fellow actors will recognize it, but the actor himself will likely not be able to explain exactly how he reached the peak of his capabilities. Our proper purpose then cannot be to lift the acting student up to the summit, but to gesture in the general direction of the top, and meanwhile set about seeing that, like a mountain climber in training, he is given as many skills and experiences as are likely to prove helpful in his essentially solitary trek upwards.

The structure of this training underscores this process of ascent. First come the basic, fundamental Exercises, for conditioning the actor's body and opening his mind to the subtleties of his physical being; then come the Explorations designed to awaken him to the medium through which he is passing and to the interaction of medium and message that provides him with the tools he will need; finally come the Applications, where we offer practice climbs so that he can test his equipment and his sense of direction. For this practice the atmosphere should be experimental (rather than success- or goal-oriented). This is still a period of discovery and most of what the actor learns he alone will know for sure.

Let us use a definition of acting to focus our remarks. Suzanne K. Langer usefully comments on the internal–external flow that lies at the heart of characterization:

> Since every utterance is the end of a process which began inside the speaker's body, an enacted utterance is a part of a virtual act, apparently springing at the moment from thought and feeling; so the actor has to create the illusion of an inward activity issuing in spontaneous speech, if his words are to make a dramatic and not a rhetoric effect.*

In the chain of events that culminates in speech we see an inextricable linkage between plain visceral activity and verbal expression. If speech does first arise in a mental act, it is only made possible through a physiological process. There are two kinds of "internal" origins, then, for cerebral articulation: the classic "internal" (emotion memory, intention, desire) and the physical internal—the body apparatus that shapes space and makes noise. Both thought and feeling are nestled within what you could call "gut" (visceral) life. This is what I call the organic reality. It is this verbal an physiological reality that stage movement training must work toward because the whole body is involved in the physiological process of communication.

I would like to take Miss Langer's statement one step further: Whereas the actor must at least create the "illusion" of inward activity, I believe that the ideal to work toward is not "the illusion of an inward activity," but rather the creation of an actual inner (or inward) reality that can be reflected outward. The illusion thus comes not from pretending that something is happening where there is nothing, but in the actor's creating an activity within himself that is real and therefore similar to the state the character must experience that an audience believes it is perceiving the reality of the character. This is the "illusion," and it has no connotation of "trickery," no hint of "let's pretend." Something *does* happen within the actor, or the applause and the accolades are (perhaps subconsciously) solely for the actor's skill and not because the audience has been touched emotionally. If an actor strives toward illusion—toward tricking the audience—he only serves to distance himself from the reality of the character and the play; he becomes a performer similar to a song and dance man. But if an actor

*Susanne K. Langer, *Feeling and Form* (New York: Charles Scribners' Sons, 1953), pp. 315–17.

creates an inner reality that an audience can perceive and that is appropriate—even necessary—for the character and his reality, then the actor can reach far deeper levels of the audience member's psyche and achieve a more lasting and truthful effect. Illusion *has* indeed played a role, but not in a self-serving or obvious manner. It is *this* illusion that a thinking audience accepts as *necessary* to the medium. Respect for the audience and his profession demands that the actor at least *aspire* to this level. If he fails to achieve an inner activity, *then* he can "fake it," but "faking it" should not be his goal. (This is certainly not Ms. Langer's intention, but the clarification needs to be made.)

Stage movement training justifiably concerns itself with aiding the actor to the outward reflection of the inner reality. But it should also aid in the creation of the inner reality because the inner reality is not just a creation of the mind, but depends to a great extent on the mind/body relationship.

It is to this goal that Applications aspire. In this portion of study I try to help the actor use the tools he has mastered to find a kinetic sense of a given character's reality based on the internal/external (mind/body) flow.

THE FORMAT FOR APPLICATIONS

All the work we will be doing in applying the Explorations to the problems of characterization will be performed on the basis of take-home assignments. The problems require too much thought and preparation to begin and end a project in class. Moreover, the actual class time can be most effectively used if all the acting students are working on carefully constructed studies. And even though each works alone, every actor is working on the same element of characterization. This arrangement also allows the discussion and analysis period to take on more significance at this stage, when it is most needed. The instructor is also freed from the role of constant supervisor and guide, and he too, then, can operate more efficiently—here as a critic and experimenter.

Step 1: Choose the Material

When the study of Applications begins, actors are instructed to find a scene from a contemporary play that has two characters close to themselves in age. Then they should pair off and decide which play and which character each will play. It usually takes very little time for each pair to decide on the play and characters because the options narrow considerably when the classics are removed from consideration (period and style is suitable for another class, but not basic movement—let's not confuse issues), and age and sex are taken into account. The scene should be relatively short and balanced in respect to character interaction (let's have no dialogue-with-a-corpse scenes) so that both parties have a relatively active role in the situation.

Step II: Work Alone

Once the play, scene, and characters are chosen, the work will at first be totally separate. There are many reasons for this: I want to focus the students' concentration on different areas than an acting teacher would ordinarily allow in "normal" scene study; I want to prevent one strong-willed actor from dictating ideas about characterization, the play, the scene, and even line readings to another actor; I want to interrupt the normal or habitual routine that actors, of necessity, fall into so that they are more open to the work of their fellow actors; I want to follow the path of development I have already explored; and so forth. But the main reason that I request actors to work in this fashion is because I wish each of them to make their own choices free from consideration of how those choices effect the other actor or the other character. This gives freedom not typical in normal scene study and frees each actor to make initial discoveries unencumbered by consideration of anyone else.

Step III: Explore Together

After each actor has had an opportunity to discover for himself the realities of his own character (the inner activity of the character), he is then in a position to nonverbally explore the situation with the other actor whose character he has observed (but not helped to) develop. Hopefully, each actor's understanding of his own character and the scene will be significantly altered or enriched by this interchange. Also, while it may help sharpen the actor's improvisational skills, it will certainly reinforce in him the need for a continuing development of inner activity or innerlife.

Step IV: Adding the Dialogue

A predetermined line reading or vocal pattern can often inhibit or retard an actor's development of a character. If the line reading imprints itself too heavily on the actor's psyche, he often finds himself incapable of making the subtle adjustments necessary to respond realistically— dynamically—to the changing nature of each performance. It may seem that to avoid such a situation I have taken elaborate precautions. That is only partially true.

It is far more accurate to say that this is an elaborate process for revealing a truth that is most elusive for many actors: The words spring from the character's perception of the situation and his attempt to effect change in it. What a person says and how he says it depends on many variables. An actor can only know *why* his character says the words he says by knowing everything he can about *who* his character is. *What* he says and *how* he says it are determined by the situation. Since we already know *what* is said, and *where* it is said, the actor must supply the rest.

This entire process is an attempt to give the actor the ability to provide answers to *who* and *why*, so that *how* happens inevitably as a result. If that does indeed occur, that actor must surely have come to some better understanding and command of his mind/body (organic) connection.

Using this process, working together must take place under supervision so that problems in the scene are not solved by discussion but by creative interaction (that is, Exploration applied to this specific problem). For beginning students it is most useful if a single character from the same play, and scene, remains the focus for the work in *all* of the applications. For an advanced actor there is some virtue in variety, shifting characters, scenes, or plays.

WORKING ALONE

Once the material is chosen and partners selected, actors are instructed to keep communication between themselves about the nature of the material to a minimum: Discussion needs to occur only in the review of specific material in a day's presentation. Even then actors should be discouraged from trying to consciously incorporate or reconcile their partner's work. I tell my actors, "Don't worry about putting it together; we'll bring it together later. You work on your character, he'll work on his, and we'll all get to the scene together."

Because both actors are moderately intelligent, working from the same script, and using the same tools under the same guidance, they can't be too far apart in their understanding of the nature of the problem after many weeks of study. Besides, each actor has the opportunity to observe his partner's work, and he (because I discourage conscious effort to incorporate this work) subliminally or instinctively develops an organic awareness of the character that evolves opposite his own. Almost all the work will be based in Essence theory, and therefore will affect each actor more deeply in a subliminal rather than conscious manner.

Actors must be familiar with the entire play. Too many actors believe they can develop a characterization based on the evidence supplied within the text of a single scene: That is an erroneous and destructive assumption. The scene is the specific focus for the actor's efforts, but the character-of-the-character is most completely revealed only by the knowledge of his actions as they are suggested by the entire script. And the scene occurs because of something that has happened previously, and has consequences that the *actor* must be at least aware of so that he understands the importance of this occurrence to the character.

That said, where do we begin?

As we did in the Explorations, here in the Applications, the path of attack is from the outside in (external to internal), and primarily for the same reasons as before: It is less demanding, builds sequentially into more and more difficult tasks, and allows the actor early "success" so that he feels relaxed, confident, and prepared for the more demanding problems involved in working from the inside out (internal to external). The first step then is for the actor to attempt to find the external elements of his character.

Physicalization of a Character

Physicalization involves many different aspects of a character's movement: how he walks, his posture, his mannerisms. Working in these elementary areas a student is actually preparing the foundation for the next areas of study, since any movement requires the certain use of space, time, and energy. This is merely a more direct and less subtle manner of approaching the task of preparing movement within a scene. Some actors may not know where to start—which is typical of the problem actors face when confronted with a new script. This exercise only tends to highlight the problem. I inform my actors, "Don't worry about it, don't think about it too hard. Read the play, make an educated guess, experiment until you feel you have something you can work with." I caution them not to try to make any irrevocable decisions. "Don't try to be right the first time. This is not a test, just a task. Your decisions could change as we continue to work on this scene—I'll be very surprised if they don't. Just try it. This is only the first crude step in assembling the composite. The first pieces of the montage or puzzle that will shift as you find other pieces."

THE CHARACTER'S WALK

1. Read the script through a few times to familiarize yourself with the play and the character.
2. Get up and move around the room or take a walk. Think about what happens to the character, what he says and does. Try to put yourself in his shoes so that it is him walking.
3. Have him walk in different situations, and then choose the one most typical of him. For instance: Is your character nervous, in a hurry, or worried most of the time? Is he slow, patient,

159

methodological, or meticulous? Is he plodding or lightfooted? Awkward or surefooted? Uncertain or athletic? You will find one that most suits your character. When you do, remember it, hold onto it. It will be part of a longer presentation.

THE CHARACTER'S POSTURE

1. From the walk, some sense of the character's typical stance should evolve. Try walking and stopping in different situations. It should become clear after only a short period of experimentation what feels most comfortable for this developing character.

2. When you feel you have found the physical center of the character (that is, the *character's* natural alignment) hold onto it and remember it. This too will be part of the presentation.

MANNERISMS

1. Experiment now by walking, stopping, and walking again. Once again try to find typical situations this character is likely to encounter, and as you do, experiment with different gestures. How does this character sit, stand up; does he scratch (what, where?); does he have facial twitches, nervous hand movements, repeated facial gestures of any kind?

2. Find two or three that the character could use and repeat them in different sequences between walking, sitting, standing, leaning, and so forth until they become reflexive to the movement pattern.

THE PRESENTATION

1. Prepare a simple presentation of these three elements that will be no more than one minute in length. The order of the presentation will be to do the Essence study, then to do realistic movement within a simple situation. This presentation should be designed to reveal your character's typical physical presence.

2. Make up a *simple* situation. For instance, the character walks into his apartment, goes to a table looking for something, thinks a moment, takes off his jacket, sits down and lights a cigarette. Or, waiting for a bus, the character deals with an umbrella, handbag, shopping bag, hat, and a bench.

3. *Don't* put any other person in the situation. *Don't* put in any dialogue. *Don't* make it a performance about some traumatic

occurrence such as "My mother just died!" *Don't* mime *anything.* If our character has an umbrella—you have an umbrella. If your character opens a door—have a door.

4. Once you have a firm grasp of the literal movement, prepare an Essence study based on the literal physicalized study. Again, the Essence should not be any elaborate or elongated dissertation showing the essence of the character's movement in varying states of joy and despair. It should be a simple, straightforward attempt to find the *essence* of the character's *typical* movement pattern. If successful, it should help to clarify the literal presentation.

5. Concentration should be on the character's physicalized presence within an ordinary or typical everyday situation. Bring this concentration into the presentation. Don't make it a performance. The key is simplicity.

The presentation can be conducted in several ways, but the most useful is for an actor to simply present his essence study once. Before any discussion, the actor should then present the literal element of the study. It may be useful for the discussion if the actor presents either (or both) the literal or Essence portion of the study again (not trying for an exact imitation of movements, but the general shape and feel should be the same). Then the rest of the class (without trying to guess the play or the character) should discuss the presentation in terms of what kind of person they felt they saw. The presenting actor should not attempt to confirm, deny, explain, or defend the presentation. This is not "What's My Line?" or charades. And it is certainly not a competition to see who can be the best at telling who his character is. There are no winners here. In this case, discussion serves as a tool for the presenter to analyze the many elements present in his development and execution of character elements. Usually, this presentation and discussion is quite rewarding for all concerned.

The essence of this exercise is simply to prepare a short study illustrating the physical image structure for your character through a careful, intellectual reading of the text and some intuitive insight. It can be based on a specific scene or any imaginary situation, such as walking into a room, sitting down to smoke, and so on. Keep your character alone, so you don't have to worry about what he does in relating to specific people. Do not worry about your character's emotional inner life at this point. Keep it an external portrait. You may know or glimpse the inner life already, but don't try now to analyze it or concentrate on feeling it. You are instead concerned with communicating the character's visible externals. You should use whatever props you need. The class will discuss and analyze the presentation, comparing their perceptions with the actor's intentions.

In physicalizing a character there are many elements that are not usually consciously considered by actors, although they profoundly influence his character choices. For instance, How does this character perceive and use Space, Time, and Energy? What are his principal emotions and how does he react to them physically?

When these and other elements of the character's inner world are explored, it will rapidly become obvious to the more serious students that this material not only radically alters their understanding of the character's external reality, but that the physicalized exterior is hollow without an immense volume of what some might consider unessential knowledge.

A space study may not be necessary after the physicalized essence is done. But for those wishing to use it the format is supplied.

USE OF SPACE

1. Prepare a study on the character's use of space. Again the study should be prepared in both literal and Essence form, and neither should exceed one minute in length. Again, this is to be representative of his typical attitude and actions regarding space. Is this character expansive in his movement or timid and small in his range of movement? Is he confident yet contained, or does he try to be unobtrusive and contained? How does your character use space?

2. Presentation will follow the format laid down in the Physical-ization of a Character: First present the Essence, then the literal.

3. Discussion again will focus on the observers' perception of the character's use of space—what kind of person do the observers think the character is (based on the presentation).

Don't let the presenter become defensive, explanatory, apologetic, or passive. It should be kept in mind that this is not a tool for analyzing the difference between perception and achievement, but for understanding and making valuable character choices.

ENERGY ESSENCE

This is, for most actors, an extremely valuable tool for character analysis. Its importance cannot be overemphasized, because the manner in which a character employs energy affects almost every other element of his behavior, and so provides a great wealth of information not as easily obtainable elsewhere.

Keep in mind that, as in music, all elements relate to each other to some degree, so that the tone of each additional study will have a kind of harmonic effect on the work preceding and following. Whereas the concentration is focused on one problem, our organic nature pushes us in the direction of harmonizing and amplifying the tones of each study that our inner nature finds resonate pleasingly with our prior understanding of the melody being created (that is, the character we are forming). Some students in their rush to find something startlingly new about their character try to overlook what they feel is mundane or a repetition of some previously discovered truth. This is not an accurate perception of the situation and it can be destructive as well. As with all things, the same truth about a character can be approached from many different directions and it is still the truth. So just because the studies may seem to the student to be too similar in their content and configuration, this is no reason to abandon that avenue of approach: Rediscovery of a truth is rewarding in itself. It is the utilization of the tool that we are concerned with here, not so much the result or the destination. Besides, if the character is to have an organic reality, the various elements he is composed of must have *some* harmony.

1. Prepare a presentation of the character's use of energy. Work this time only on the Essence. Don't prepare any realistic study to pair up with the Essence.

2. After the essence has been presented, ask the actor "Now let me see you—as your character would." Pause. "Good. Let's see the essence again."

Note: The specific instruction to a student should be different from the one before so that students must react spontaneously to the suggestion. Suggestions could be: "... walk around the room ..."; "...go pick up that sweater and put it on ..."; "... take off your shoes ..."; "...comb your hair ...", and so on.

3. Discussion should focus on which primary energy qualities this character uses (see Energy Qualities, in the Explorations, Chapter 4), and whether or not the feeling of the Essence was carried through to the realistic or literal movement. Also, is there evidence that the character's internal energy quality is at variance with his external image? Was the presentation organic?

Some actors have asked me to demonstrate what I want from them in class. Outside the exercises I refuse to do this because it encourages imitation. Also, the only real learning any actor achieves is in his own discoveries. I will at times supply very brief examples of how some theory might work. Here is one based on energy:

If you use Chief Bromden from "One Flew Over the Cuckoo's Nest" the energy *essence* will be ponderous and tentative. Probably sustained, meticulously controlled small movements, set into a simple repetitive pattern, interrupted with sudden jerkless pauses would typify the Chief. Then in the *realistic* portrait you would probably want to use the broom the Chief is always carrying. From a position of watchful stillness, move to the broom, pick it up and sweep with it, stop, watch, put it down, and watch again is probably the sequence you would use.

The essence or abstracted portrait helps free the body so it can move into the center of the character's physical orientation, and will ease the sense of the character's follow through; the realistic portrait is thus built on the organic base of the essence study.

ANIMAL ESSENCE:
(INTERNAL AND EXTERNAL)

Nearly every acting teacher has used and advised the approach to characterization through animal studies. Many directors have even structured a set of characterizations on the analogy of a zoo, in which each actor conceives as his part through a specific animal. The problem in acting always involves the leap from oneself to that of another character, and animals prove to be excellent bridges.

In these Applications we use animal images to move into the individual nature of a person. Note, however, that the animal quality within an actor or character usually takes different movement shapes from those of the literally observed animal. Even in *The Hairy Ape* by Eugene O'Neill the title role, although perhaps portrayed by an apelike bulk of a man, does not literally imitate apelike movements. This would be ridiculous and trite. But the use of the animal image can be quite beneficial and has a strong relationship to use of energy.

Probably, while there are many people who look or act just like a certain animal, perhaps their own pet, there are few who look *and* act just like that animal. Also, we say a person behaves just like a sloth, a snake, or a magpie, but very likely he bears no physical resemblance to that animal. Once in a while a very graceful, lithe, independent, narcissistic individual comes along, and we have our perfect "cat." More often, we must conceive of people, unlikely as it seems, in terms of combinations. He looks like_____(externally) but behaves just like a_____(internally). So we have a strange breed of crossed strains, dog-toads, bear-bats, rooster-lions. In this section we will experiment with looking at characters in terms of these combined animals (unless your character is the perfect lizard, elephant, or_____).

1. Prepare a four-part presentation of your character. You will first show what animal he is externally, in his essence; then follow with a realistic version of his external movement. Then (here is where most characters demand a switch in animal

models), do an abstracted version of his inner animal nature, and end with a realistic exhibit of the character's movement.

2. Try to prepare smooth transitions between step one and two, two and three, and so forth, until you are not dropping the characterization momentarily.

3. Discussion should focus on the qualities of the various essences, what there was in the animal that seemed to fit the character externally or internally, whether the quality of the essence carried over into the realistic, and so on.

TIME ESSENCE

The last basic element essential to all movement is time, and it is the one that most lures out the intellectual in actors. This is not an intellectually-based Application. It may be intellectually stimulating, but the focus for actors or students at this time should be on the kinetic feeling the character's use of time promotes. By this time the actor should not have to be cautioned not to overanalyze or overintellectualize any exercise. He is, if he has applied himself seriously, becoming aware and gaining control of the organic reality of mind and body within himself so that inspiration springs from an unidentifiable source—not just the mind.

This is the technique that will yield most fruit, and needs to be further encouraged, especially at this point. The "mind" most people identify is the conscious mind. And actors are no exception to the rule; many bow down before the conscious process. But as artists—creators, they should know that the conscious process is only a small portion of the mind, and they must learn to trust the many other levels on which they function to help them find the answers they seek.

In this case the question is, "How does your character use time?" If we phrase the question in that manner, however, the student will "think." So rather than ask a question, I give an order: "Find the rhythm Essence of your character." Now the actor is motivated to *act*, and actors are never so creative as when they actively commit themselves to pursuit. Therein lies the genius we as movement teachers seek to arouse. If further instructions are necessary about how to proceed, I tell actors, "Don't think about meter, or tempo, or accent, or defining anything. Find a quiet space and do your own movement exploration. Trust your instincts and the work that has preceded this, and the essence will shape itself for you. When you find the rhythm, explore it in every part of the body, and find what feels most typical or natural for the character."

Students should know by now, from exploring their own rhythm, that rhythmic pattern will vary depending on external and internal changes. What we are looking for here, however, is the NORM.

1. Find the rhythm Essence of your character.

2. Prepare a two-part study that will flow from the essence to the literal.

3. For this presentation, try to find a series of literal movements your character would probably do *in the scene.*

4. Prepare the presentation so that the Essence flows into the literal, and the literal flows back into the Essence so that the entire study is constructed: Essence, Literal, Essence.

5. Partners follow each other as before with discussion happening after both partners in a scene have presented their studies.

EMOTIONAL THREAD

Perhaps the most powerful of all the actor's tools in terms of understanding and performing the character is emotion. It is often a misunderstood and misused tool, but it can also be very effective. This application of emotion through Essence work should help to clarify many areas about the scene and about the character.

1. For the purposes of this exercise, assume that there are at most three to five major emotions one character experiences in a scene. There may be many smaller, finer, more subtle emotions, but choose just the strongest, most vivid emotions the character seems to experience. Envision these emotions as beads or knots on the time line of the scene. They are the backbone of the character's reaction to episodes that occur as the scene progresses.

2. Once you have chosen the major emotions in the scene, tie them together in sequence in your mind so that they can come to mind without your consciously thinking "OK, that was hate, now what's next? Oh ya. Disgust. Here's disgust." Try to make them flow one into another naturally, so that there is some transition for you from one to another.

3. Then when you feel you understand how the mechanics operate, prepare an essence of each individual emotion. When you have an acceptable essence for each one, use the transitions you have found to tie each emotion to the next so that they form one long smoothly flowing Essence study of the major emotions the character experiences in the scene.

4. Presentation will be executed as follows: Partners will go one after another. Each person does his entire Essence study twice without pause for discussion until both partners in a single scene have completed their presentation.

5. Discussion is open-ended in terms of topics class members can discuss, but as a general rule, two or three minutes at the most is all the time that need be spent for any scene.

As you can see, the progress of the Applications is beginning to move in the direction of the actors working together. It is still premature for them to rehearse together, however, and discussion outside the classroom can be more destructive than constructive at this point. Although actors at this time are beginning to assemble the framework of the scene subliminally, the organic awareness they are developing can easily be disrupted by intellectual interference.

Now that the actor has answered basic questions about the character (who, what, when, where, why) he is ready to explore the material in the scene with his partner.

EXPLORE TOGETHER: MOVEMENT IN A SCENE

All the effort thus far has been focused toward this time in the process. This is when the fruit should begin to ripen for actor and teacher alike, when the discipline begins to become enjoyable, and the work becomes creation. Here is where the tools of improvisation, essence, and movement terminology merge with two actors skilled in the same school of thought in the same scene, and a shared experience of each other's independent development of character.

Actors are usually more than eager at this point to begin this next stage of application of accumulated technique and theory. They should also be ready to begin completion of their sense of their own organic reality. Dialogue will be interjected gradually as part of this process, and will, in a sense, be deemphasized so that the focus and development stays not on the words or ideas, but on the commitment to maintaining a sense of the scene as an organism's response to an evolving situation. Memorization of lines is destructive to this process, so I discourage that process. In the end the lines will be there—complete and exact, but not from preconception as is typical in the theatre. Hopefully, the words will come naturally from the situation—spontaneously and not pre-meditatively. Hopefully, the dialogue will spill out of the joint explorations as a result of an inner activity, and not as an intellectually inspired desire to achieve a startlingly effective performance.

This is the goal. And to reach it, it is important to maintain the sense of natural forward momentum we've been trying to establish. In this book, and by this introduction, I have tried to provide clear delineation between significant portions of work, including this one. But in the classroom the importance of this phase of work should not be highlighted. Actors tend to become self-consciious when one says, "What you are doing is significant," because they begin to overintellectualize once again.

There is in the material as I have designed it an apparent flow, a steady adding on, a progressive acquisition of skills. This is no less true for the Applications. It is important for the teacher to know, however, the value and subtlety of this last portion of classroom activity, and to provide a sense of steady forward momentum rather than to suggest quantum leaps in significance of effort.

Not much has changed after all: Actors will work with each other only under controlled classroom situations and not at all outside the classroom until the very end; this is still a period of exploration and experimentation (something actors get precious little of in this high-pressure, judgment-oriented profession); and the addition of the voice is, after all, only the natural, logical inclusion of what really amounts to another physical instrument—another part of the organic whole that is the actor. Interestingly, if one is working in a conservatory situation, where acting and voice with movement are taught simultaneously and separately by qualified specialists, by the time the actor is asked to incorporate the use of his vocal instrument in his explorations, he should have gained sufficient control and command of his voice that the incorporation of the two will be an efficient and natural release rather than an effort.

But, we are ahead of ourselves. Let's start this newest portion of work at its beginning: without words, without sound; with essense alone. Then we can build from there.

Energy Essence of the Scene

1. Go back to the script of the scene. This time I want you to find the Energy Essence of the scene. Answer these questions first: How does your character use energy in the scene? Does his use or application of energy change? (It usually will several times.)

2. Prepare your Essence of your character's use of energy in the scene only.

3. Presentation:
   a. Partners will follow one another. As soon as one partner finishes presenting his Essence without comment, the other partner will perform his while the first person sits with the rest of the class.
   b. Then, before *any* comment, both partners should go onto the floor and lie down and relax. They are then guided through the rest of the Exploration by the voice commands of the teacher.
   c. "Close your eyes. Relax. Clear yourself. Breathe deeply and empty your mind." (Pause) "Now bring your concentration onto your Energy Essence. Try to feel your body moving in the Essence movement, but do not move." (Pause) "Fill yourself with the situation of the scene and try to let that effect the growing sensation of the Energy Essence." (Pause) "When you feel ready, begin to move with the Essence." (Pause) "Start alone, but begin to react to the other person. Allow the other presence to alter

your Essence. Free yourselves from your planned series of movements. Be spontaneous. Don't plan it. Let it happen."

d. When the actors have explored, but not exhausted the possibilities (or themselves) "Follow through with what you are doing. Then let go of your action and relax back onto the floor. Don't just drop off. Finish what you're doing." (Pause) "Relax. Breathe deeply. Release all your tension. Clear yourself. Bring yourself back to a neutral state." (Pause) "Good. Sit up and we'll talk about it."

e. Discussion:
"How did you feel about the exploration?"
"What did you find?"
"Anyone from the class have a comment?"
"Thank you. Good. Next."

It is important in these explorations of the scene to try to keep both actors in the essence work. At times one or the other or both will begin what I call indicating (that is, they mime "I feel bad" or "Don't hurt me, pretty please?" or "Let's have fun"), and when this happens positive results are impossible. The work becomes shallow, hollow, undisciplined, uncentered, not organic—and no one can take it seriously. If it happens, strong measures are needed to point up the fact so that work on other scenes is not destroyed by this kind of errant application of effort.

It shouldn't happen too frequently in Energy, but because of the increasingly subtle and fragile nature of the ensuing work, and the addition of voice and dialogue, there is an ever greater danger of this occurring. That is why early detection and treatment of the problem is necessary and helpful.

Animal Essence with the Scene

1. Refresh and review your internal and external Animal Essence studies. Bring them to class tomorrow.
2. Presentation:
   a. Partners follow one another. As soon as Partner A finishes both internal and external essence studies, Partner B will present his.
   b. Now both of you relax onto the floor and clear yourself.
   c. Relax. Breathe easily in and out. Clear yourself. Listen to the whole explanation of what I want you to do before you begin. Choose one of your animal essences, it doesn't matter which one, and concentrate on filling yourself with the feeling it brings to you. Fill yourself with the situation of the scene, and allow yourself to move (with the essence you are using) in that situation.

d. When you are ready, begin relating to the other person in essence.
e. If you feel comfortable and committed, you can allow yourself to use dialogue. Keep in the essence movement, and don't worry about the lines from the script.
f. Take your time, and don't begin until you're ready. Don't think about it. You're on your own now. Begin when you're ready.

At this point there are many different avenues that may be followed and each depends on where the actors lead each other in the exploration. This first time the dialogue may be stilted, or awkward, or halting. If they are really into the essence, however, it may be quite stirring and effective. Success should be warmly rewarded. Those failing should be warmly encouraged, and the source of the problem pinpointed if possible. It will be obvious to everyone where the exercise was effective and where it was not. Some scenes may be very verbose; in others, hardly a verbal interchange wil occur. This is to be expected. Neither is "right." But regardless of which path is taken, the exploration should end the same way.

g. "Good. Follow through with what you are doing. Let go of dialogue. Go back into the essence alone. Take your time, don't just break off." (Pause) "Release your tension. Relax onto the floor." (Pause) "Clear yourself. Bring yourself back to a neutral state. Relax."
h. Discussion:
"Good."
"Sit up and let's talk about it."
"How do you feel?"
"What did you find?"
"How did you respond to the addition of dialogue?"

It is quite normal for one or two scenes to have some seemingly difficult problem with the first addition of dialogue. Usually one or two scenes will seem to "click," but the majority of scenes will go in and out of it so that no great experience is forthcoming. It is important for everyone to understand that some scenes and some individuals work better with different focus of activity. A seeming failure here is not catastrophic unless we allow it to be. It is just as important at this point for the actors to understand how this effort *can* be rewarding—just as much as it is to succeed. Scenes that "succeed" this time may "fail" the next; others that "fail" now may "succeed" later.

It is also important to understand that the terms "success" and "failure" are not relevant to this work, and such concepts form a block to future effort. Even if the terms had some merit in this training, it would be over the long term—only at the end of the training period could such determinations be made. You could use the battle/war analogy—won the battle but lost the war—lost the battle but won the war—or even, as in the case of the Romans and the Greeks, when the Romans "lost every battle and won the war." "Victory" and "defeat" for the student, like "success" and "failure," are true measures of no lasting reality.

Even that analogy is inaccurate, however, because there is no opponent and no losing involved. Each student will gain (has already gained up to this point), it is only a matter of how much is gained; and no one can judge that because the effects of this training are quite likely to be more evident long after student and teacher have parted company.

So, do not linger over success or failure, but reinforce the concept that this is a period of exploration and discovery, not a performance. Do not allow contemplation of it, but force the students to rush headlong into the next project.

Counterpoint, Conflict, Yin-Yang

This next project requires actors to analyze the text of the scene in terms of the major conflict in the scene. All drama is based on conflict—without it drama does not exist. There are many different ways to conceptualize the problem. Here are several supporting images one can use to define it.

COUNTERPOINT

As in the discussions and explorations of Time, counterpoint represents a situation in which there are two contrasting sets of elements, in this case, two people with contrasting or opposing desires.

CONFLICT

Conflict is the clash of wills within a scene. In human relationships, will exerts an almost ever-present force. It is sometimes very weak or seemingly nonexistent, but it is a basic force that keeps human beings (perhaps all living things) alive. We use our will in even the most basic of voluntary functions, but nowhere is the application of will any stronger as when a human being is faced with the obstacle of another contradictory and competing will. This is what makes for good drama—the clash of wills. Conflict.

YIN-YANG

One of the primary principles in one of the oldest existing forms of religion/philosophy, Taoism, is that the universe is one thing, composed of contradictory elements. No element can exist without its opposite also existing. This operates on many levels, but in no other discipline is the concept more readily applicable than here in scene work.

Simply then, if one character in the scene desires one outcome, the other character *must* desire a totally contradictory outcome.

For this tool to be effective, of course, both characters' wills and efforts must be of great magnitude, and both must be extremely resourceful in their attempt to achieve the outcome they desire. This brings about conflict and provides counterpoint in the scene. This may not be true of every two-person scene in drama, but for any scene worthy of prolonged exploration the concept can be a formidable tool for unlocking the secrets within it.

With these three images to draw from, student and teacher alike should very quickly see the prospects for application of the concept. Actors should be given the problem several days before the presentation is to be made, so that there is sufficient time for each individual to clearly and succinctly state *the* major conflict of the scene and to prepare an Essence study of it. Partners should *not* discuss it, because one strong-willed actor could force his view and concept of the scene and problem on an unwilling and therefore uncommitted comrade. *The* major conflict should be simple enough to pinpoint, but different actors and different characters have seemingly different ways of verbally expressing or even conceiving the same problem.

Fortunately, the actors won't be spelling out the problem verbally, but relating it directly through the Essence. Each Essence will alter the other slightly, but neither partner is thus able to dictate terms; therefore, both are surprised and hopefully, more spontaneous in the resulting improvisation. Here is the way it will work on the day of presentation:

1. Both partners onto the floor, lay down and relax. Clear yourselves. Let go of all your tension. Breathe deeply.

2. Now, review the scene in your mind's eye, trying to visualize it in terms of ther major conflict. Build your reaction to that conflict as though it were you who faced the problem. Let it touch you personally.

3. Let the feeling grow until you have to express your feeling in terms of the Essence. Don't rush it or force it. Let it happen naturally.

4. When you begin, use the Essence to express your emotion.

5. If you feel comfortable with it, you can use dialogue. Don't worry about lines. Improvise on the scene using the Essence conflict as your focus.

6. Good. Follow through with what you are doing, and then let the tension drain from you and let yourself relax onto the floor as the conflict drains away from you. Relax. Breathe deeply. Bring yourself back to a neutral state, letting go of all tension, all problems drain out of you onto the floor. Just relax.

7. Good. Sit up easily, open your eyes. How do you feel? All right, let's talk about it. What did you find? Does this help you with your character? The scene?

Please note that only the general shape of verbal commands is listed here. Much depends on how the actors respond to when and what is specifically said. But it is obvious that this is a departure from the established technique of one person presents, the other presents, then they explore together. Although one could use that technique here, this shock treatment of both actors unaware of and unprepared for the shape of each other's essence, is far more effective, and the results usually quite startling.

In a later Application using this technique it is sometimes quite useful for actors to move from the Essence to Essence-with-dialogue to dialogue-with-realistic-movement without halting, pausing, or conscious deliberation.

For most classes, this will be too soon to use the technique, but advanced classes or a team that is especially tuned in may inspire me to suggest it during their exploration. Even when the suggestion is not verbalized, however, the movement may tend to become more naturalized due to the nature of the problem, so the transition into realistic movement is far easier than it sounds. It is so natural a process that some partners try to make the transition too quickly, and it sometimes takes a gentle reminder to stay with the Essence movement.

Major Intentions of the Scene

Intention is another concept frequently used in the craft of acting to help focus the actor's efforts in rehearsal and performance. Its definition and use is fairly standard in today's theatre, but it never hurts to spell out the precise use of any term to a group of people expected to understand and use it in the same way.

Briefly then, intention defines a particular type of application of will. In this theatrical context, an intention is a conscious design by one person to achieve a desired reaction in another person. It can most succinctly be defined by a statement declaring your intention toward another person.

I want to ...

... impress her

... make him feel guilty.

... hurt him.

... make her feel sorry for me.

... entice her.

173

... make him proud of me.

... confuse him.

... make her feel ridiculous.

... etc.

These are subtextual statements that must be supplied by the actor, and help to focus an entire series of lines. This is sometimes referred to as a "beat," which is a concise way of describing a small passage of dialogue that centers on one small, clearly defined element of contention within a scene.

Of course, you cannot play an entire scene with one intention. That would be ridiculous. Usually there are between four and six major intentions, and the actor needs to spell this out for himself. That is what this Application is designed to facilitate.*

Now that we all know how the term is being used in this context, let's see if we can find a way to translate the intellectual description into some meaningful organic context. This is not too difficult to do because the method of translation is the Essence Study.

1. Prepare an Essence study, independently of your partner, of the major intentions of your character in the scene you're working on.

2. Do not be concerned about what the other character is doing. Concentrate only on finding and preparing an Essence study of the four or five major intentions of your character. (You may have less or more, but this is unlikely if the scene is well written.)

3. Don't discuss this with your partner. There is no need for any kind of prior understanding agreement about "who does what to whom at which time for which reason." That's what you will discover in the exploration of the scene.

When the actors have had time to sort these things out for themselves, the presentation will take on a slightly different shape.

4. Presentation:
    a. Partners again will follow one another, but after each presentation there will be a *brief* pause to discuss each actor's study.

Caution: Some actors confuse "intention" with "objective." Objective is an entirely different concept that refers to the ultimate goal of the character in the scene. For instance, a young man may have the objective: "To make my mother admit and repent her sins," but in the attempt to achieve that goal, he may have several different intentions: "I want to ... shock her ... embarrass her ... make her feel disgust with herself ... etc." This in fact happens in Act III, Scene IV of Shakespeare's *Hamlet*.

The essence should be clear enough so that the rest of the class can identify each intention. Of course, no one can expect the class to express their interpretation in the same verbatim manner as the person presenting the essence, but some synonymous approximation for each intention is possible. If this were not so, no meaningful joint exploration could take place. If the class is unable to identify the changes in even a rough approximation, it is evident that the presenter has not adequately specified the intentions. If this is true, he does not know what his character intends, so how can he fulfill that intention? This forces actors to make a choice, and provides a means of detecting whether or not they have. The question of whether it is the "right" choice or whether it is appropriate for the character is not important at this point. What is important is that the actor make a strong choice and find and commit himself to the essence.

b.   After both actors partnering in a scene have presented their intention study, they should do an exploration together.

c.   The joint exploration will begin with both actors using the essence studies as a starting point, and then, when they are ready, they should make the transition into dialogue with essence movement, and then into realistic movement with dialogue.

Discussion afterwards can involve any area of special interest aroused by the process, but observation should be noted about whether or not the organic movement of the essence carried through to the realistic and dialogue. Often actors will begin to "indicate," leaving behind most internal organic sense of commitment, and begin to "pretend" or perform. This is the antithesis of the concept we are working for here, and if I perceive this happening in the joint exploration, I will usually stop it soon after and begin the discussion earlier than I would normally, trying to gently, but pointedly, highlight the destructiveness of this tendency for the actors involved.

It can provide an extremely valuable learning experience if I am forced to do this, because then we have an immediate example I can use to illustrate the observation: "Can you see the difference between when they were committed to and concentrated in organic movement, and when they came out of it and started indicating?" It is a rhetorical question only in the sense that no one ever fails to see, so obvious is the contrast to both observer and participant.

The fascinating thing about the process is that (in spite of the fact that students have not been instructed to "memorize the lines") in explorations in which the organic commitment stays constant throughout, students will be stunned by their almost flawless verbatim execution. It would take too long to explain why I think this happens, but the fact that it does is enough to make believers of some residual skeptics I have found in some of my classes at this point in the training. It is not magic or supernatural in any sense. Rather, I believe it is the most natural occurrence given the type and intensity of analysis students have used on the script.

Emotional Thread within the Scene

Since the Emotional Thread has already been covered in this chapter, and for the student it will have been relatively recently, each actor should have a good grasp of the concept and perhaps even the Essence study in his kinetic memory. All that is necessary now is to ask actors to review and renew, if necessary, the Essence of Emotional Thread.

The same procedure for presentation as has just been initiated should be used, or one of the previous methods explained may be returned to depending on the class' needs and abilities. The procedure described in the previous step is by far the most effective, however, and should be used if at all possible. Less elaborate explanations to each pair will be necessary.

The class will be informed about the format to be used and the following admonition should be all that is necessary.

1. Lie down. Relax. Clear yourself.
2. Fill yourself with the Essence study and the feeling of the scene. Begin only when you're ready. Take your time. Don't force anything, just try to hold onto the truth of the scene. Begin when you're ready.

The same discussion technique can be used, and depending on the nature of the class and the scenes presented, a wide variety of object lessons, conclusions, and illustrations can be made. This is the time when teaching this class is a joyfully creative experience, because most individuals will have by this time broken through the more mundane and fundamental barriers of faulty conceptualizing, physical blocks, defensiveness, and so forth. They are a solid group of awakening craftsmen, challenging themselves, each other, and their teacher with the strength of their discoveries and creative energies. Most individuals are growing confident of their new sense of organic unity, and it may be difficult to keep the forward momentum as steady, and even as it needs to be to ensure that all the members of the class move forward together.

The next step is, after all, only the next logical step on the developmental ladder.

Working Together Outside Class

Depending on how much time is remaining to the class, there are a variety of ways in which to proceed. Probably the most valuable is to use the following technique to further develop the sense of realistic organic movement in a scene:

1. Review and refurbish your _____Essence study. (Any of the Essence studies could work for this; the most effective, however, may be Emotion, Counterpoint, Intention, Energy, or Animal Essences. Students should choose the one they feel will best aid them in solving problems they have encountered with the scene.)

2. Meet outside of class time with your partner and, using the Essence study, do your own exploration of the scene.

3. Prepare a realistic version of the scene using the universal elements you found in the exploration.

4. Bring it to class and present first the exploration; then the realistic versions. (Set up the realistic set before you start the presentation. Make sure you have placed any prop and all furniture you *need* for the action in the scene. That way you can move right from the essence into the realistic without a break. This allows you to keep the organic connection established from the essence when you move into the scene. Don't mime anything. This will break the organic connection.)

5. Discussion will center on the ability to carryover the organic and universal elements from the Essence to the realistic, as well as your perception of the discoveries you made in working this way.

Although this particular format could be used alternately with each Essence study, there may not be enough class time for more than one or two of them.

ANALYZING APPLICATIONS

Application of any theory should lend itself to analysis. This is no less true of the theory of organic movement through use of Essence work. How does one analyze it? What terms do you use?

Generally, the same tools of analysis are used in this case that are used in any theatrical or experimental presentation: Based on what we can see and hear, are we convinced of the sincerity, commitment, and reality of the people involved? Were they organically involved, and not just "play-acting"? Did they involve me in the problem or the situation? Did I understand generally the nature of the situation or problem? Was it appropriate to the nature of the scene or characters? Did they find or experience anything worthwhile?

The last question can only be answered by the people actually involved in the presentation. The other questions can be answered by either observer or presenter in many cases. Not everyone will agree in every case about the correctness of the choices, but anyone can readily see the degree of commitment, concentration, and focus present in an essence application. If there were a great focus and concentration and a high level of commitment to the exploration of the problem, comprehension and appreciation of the universal elements within the presentation should be a simple matter.

To help illustrate this I have provided a short series of photographs highlighting two such explorations each from two scenes being developed by students from one of my movement for actors courses at the University of Connecticut in the 1982 spring semester. The two scenes were evolved over the course of the entire fifteen-week semester. Therefore they should be of a fair enough quality to be analyzed. Although it is a difficult assignment to capture the "essence of an Essence" in just a few still photographs, it is the best method available in book format because of the length of the exploration.

All four sets of photographs are arranged in the proper chronological order and were taken while the exploration unfolded so that none were "posed" shots. Two sets of photographs correspond to Animal Essence Explorations (one exploration using animal essences from each scene), one set corresponds to an Emotional Essence Exploration, and one to an Intention Essence Exploration.

The Indian Wants the Bronx by **Israel Horowitz**

> Murphy: Jim Sheerin
> Joey: Gary Chase

Note: To simplify matters, rather than using both the actor's names and the character's names, I will simply refer to the character.

ANIMAL ESSENCE EXPLORATION

In this series of photographs (Figures 5–1 to 5–6) we see the concentration and fine focus necessary to any theatrical mode. These actors are awake and alert to the minutest changes in each other's actions. Their minds are actively involved in problem solving. While their movements are not literal, they are relating to each other on an abstract, or essence, plane.

It is obvious that their movements are not intended or shaped to be realistic in form, nor are they "imitations" of animal movements, or even "miming" movements indicating any intellectualized message. These actors are obviously engaged in an entirely different kind of activity. The movement does seem to flow from the center, and it appears to have a certain amount of follow-through.

If any negative criticism could be leveled at this Exploration, it is perhaps that the movement does not seem to be specific enough in terms of the character's intentions toward each other. But then, that was not the focus of this Exploration. The focus was Internal/External Animal Essences as they shaped the scene. What were they?

FIGURE 5-1

FIGURE 5-2

FIGURE 5-3

FIGURE 5-4

FIGURE 5-5

FIGURE 5-6

Murphy (wearing dark shirt, sweat pants, and socks)
    External Animal—Ferret
    Internal Animal—Cougar

Joey (wearing light shirt, black pants, and in bare feet)
    External Animal—a little fiesty dog
    Internal Animal—a small, starving rat

One would expect, given those choices, that whereas Joey may begin as the aggressor, or at least as aggressive as Murphy, that Murphy would eventually come to dominate his weaker adversary. This indeed seems to happen. If other choices were made by both actors, and this result did not occur, the choices would have to be wrong, because this is what happens in the script. But for these actors, these choices were good ones, as we can see from their use of them in this Exploration.

Compare this result with the same scene explored with the use of Intention.

INTENTION ESSENCE EXPLORATION

In this series of photographs (see Figures 5–7 to 5–12) we quickly see that both characters are relating far more specifically to each other. The focus, commitment, and concentration are just as strong as it was in the previous exploration of the same scene, but the movements are now very different even though the quality of the movement stays very much the same.

The same relationship between the two characters is translated into action without dialogue from an entirely different direction. Murphy is still dominant, even though Joey begins intending things to be different. Murphy's intentions are strong longer and seem even to grow in strength as Joey begins to weaken or tire in the battle of wills.

Notice that while there is physical contact, neither *actor* intends any hurt to the other, whereas the characters may, and in this case, do intend harm (perhaps only mental) to the other character. This is the First Law of Improvisation:

> "Thou shalt not cause, nor intend to cause, physical harm to another *actor*, regardless of provocation."

In this way, we an insure a maximum degree of safety for all participants, regardless of the apparent violence intended by one *character* to another.

This is another way in which the Essence Explorations perform a valuable service. One character may "intend" to crush another and because of the restraint of both the First Law of Improvisation and the requirement not to be literal in expression, the actor has two forms of conditioning against what may be a regrettable loss of control under less structured circumstances.

At any rate, although this series of photos may appear to show a violent struggle, what it really reveals, upon closer examination, are two

FIGURE 5-7

FIGURE 5-8

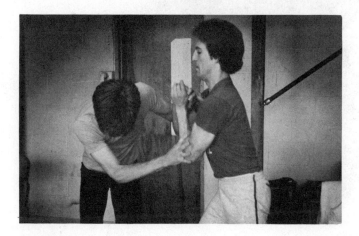

FIGURE 5-9

FIGURE 5-10

FIGURE 5-11

FIGURE 5-12

characters locked in a battle of wills, which two *actors* (who are cooperating in a very professional manner) are striving to explore and express through nonliteral or Essence movement. This is no attempt at illusion. It is not a game. Neither actor is attempting to "win" anything. They are working together to find the truth of the scene.

In this case, the exploration seems to have yielded even more fruit because although the general shape of the scene has remained the same as before, the new focus has provided for more active choices to be made. Also, the same physical relationship that was discovered in the Animal Essence Exploration has been retained in a slightly altered form, thus adding to the richness of this exploration.

The Wager by Mark Medoff
Leeds: Robert Phillips
Ward: Geoffrey Dawes

ANIMAL ESSENCE EXPLORATION

In this series of photographs (see Figures 5–13 to 5–20) it is even easier to see the effects of the animal images. Even without knowing the actors' choices, one can almost pinpoint the type of animals and the actors' attitudes toward them. It is easier here to see how these choices relate to the scene and how the characters relate to each other. The choices are strong and specific and the actions reflect an entirely different dynamic that is appropriate to the scene.

There is a lack of physical violence in the literal scene, but there is an emotional fire storm that evolves. This is mirrored in the exploration; even though the focus is on the seemingly mundane problem of internal/external animal essences. What were they?

Leeds—(wearing white T-shirt and light sweatpants)
External—big, tired, sleepy, floppy-eared dog
Internal—cobra

Ward—(wearing dark T-shirt and dark sweatpants)
External—ape
Internal—ape

Analysis here is even simpler than in the last scene's Animal Essence Exploration. Here, given the choices that the actors made, one would have to assume that Leeds' sleepy dog would be a natural enticement for the curiosity of Ward's ape. This happens. One would also expect that the ape, in his attempt to figure out, or toy with the dog, would annoy, arouse, and cause the cobra to strike. This also happens.

While it is obvious, however, the movements seem to have follow-through and flow from an organic base. The essence appears to have served these actors very well.

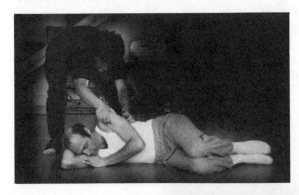

FIGURE 5-13

FIGURE 5-14

FIGURE 5-15

FIGURE 5-16

FIGURE 5-17

FIGURE 5-18

FIGURE 5-19

FIGURE 5-20

EMOTIONAL ESSENCE EXPLORATION

To this series of photographs (see Figures 5–21 to 5–25) two things are immediately obvious: First, this exploration is far more active and "violent" than the last one; second, the general shape so closely resembles the other that one could tell they belong together even if there were no descriptive passage to explain the fact.

Emotional Essence in a Scene

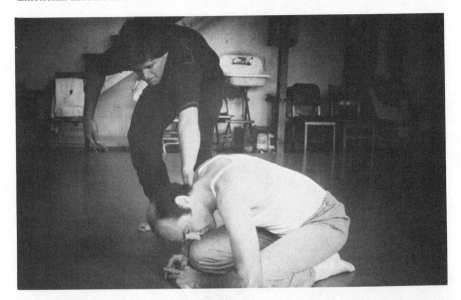

FIGURE 5-21

FIGURE 5-22

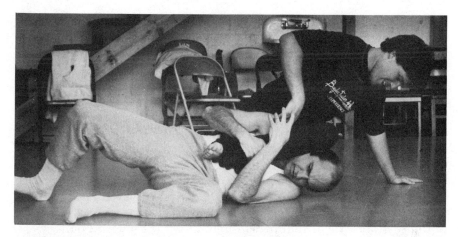

FIGURE 5-23

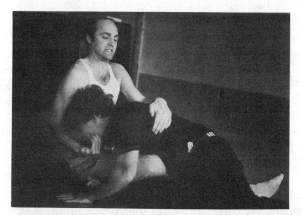

FIGURE 5-24

FIGURE 5-25

Why is this exploration so much more violent? Obviously, the focus on emotions has aroused the natural emotion already "programmed" into the actors' concept of the scene. This produces a more volatile reaction, similar to lifting the weight rocking on the outlet valve of a steam kettle.

Why is the general shape of the two explorations so close? Probably because it is "right" for the scene in their minds. It is a good thing that they feel free from the need to "find something new" in an area that feels so much like the truth to them.

What else can we say about this Exploration? Commitment, focus, concentration are all present and used to good purpose. The actors are obviously organically involved, and if one weren't aware of the basic nature of this battle of wills and involved in or engaged by it, that fact would say more about that person than about the presentation.

Perhaps the only negative comment one might make is that both these explorations look more like a wrestling match than an exploration of basic character elements as they apply to a scene. If that observation is true, the actors will have largely wasted their energy in this effort, only to engage in a test of one actor's physical prowess as opposed to another's.

In defense of this particular case, however, I can testify to the high professional awareness and commitment of both actors, and because of the nature of the *movement* (as opposed to these still frames, which may suggest quite the contrary) I witnessed, that this was not the case. *In this case* the actors involved cooperated with each other in a violent-appearing contest while exploring the emotional realities of their characters in the scene.

Although this may seem to some like hairsplitting, it is not. Learning is at stake. Health is at stake. Personal and professional good will rises and falls on the ability of actors to differentiate between their own and their character's desires and emotions. And we should take advantage of every opportunity that presents itself to make this distinction.

Discussion

Now compare the general shape of one scene to the next, one study to the next. There are some universal qualities common to all well-written two-person scenes in drama (discounting, of course, the well-written scenes describing the happy fortune of two people in total harmony and such). In each series of photographs, note the escalating nature of the confrontation leading naturally toward a climax. This also demands, in most cases, a winner. Note how the aggressor or dominant role seems to change through the course of the explorations. Sometimes the dominance will shift back and forth several times, but if it *never* shifts there seems to be far less dramatic potential.

One can use all these methods of analysis (and many more) to understand, evaluate, or dissect these explorations. The purpose of the explorations (indeed, of this entire training process) should be the guide, however, in all discussion. The goal is to develop within each actor the ability to find and maintain organic movement in every character he assumes on stage by helping him to develop his own mind/body connection, thus reducing the gap between impulse and action to practical invisibility, and providing him with rehearsal and performance tools to achieve his purpose.

CONCLUSION

Although each area of study provides its own rewards to various students at various times, the period of study that seems to be the most rewarding is toward the end of the Applications. This is probably because the results of all the long effort become more and more obvious. Because of the new physical fitness and kinesthetic awareness, students are so much better prepared to follow their creative impulses that they are no longer inhibited by their misconceptions about their bodies' capabilities. They have a firm grasp of a reliable set of tools that they know how to use to answer more questions about their characters than they knew how to ask before. The gap between impulse and action is nearly nonexistent because of their awareness and command of the organic unity of mind and body. They now know, from firsthand experience, that what the body does has shape and substance in the mind and that no matter how the mind functions, the body naturally functions in like manner—automatically, spontaneously, *naturally* mirroring or relaxing the inner reality of the mind. They know it from their own experience. They've seen how it functions in others.

They trust this knowledge and because they trust it and understand it, they can begin to command it to serve them. When a teacher can see this happen, it is an incredibly rewarding experience. When a student feels his own command, it is also quite a reward for the amount of hard work he has put in, and it reinforces his confidence and belief in his abilities.

But we must keep in mind that it *is* long and hard work. It is the long periods of struggle followed by sudden awareness of progress and the many small breakthroughs that provide the platform for this success—if we can call it success.

As I have said before, "success" and "failure" have no lasting value in this context. But if they do, their measure is, at best, defined in relativistic terms (that is, "He has improved a great deal in this and that respect" or "She has grown incredibly from that first day when ..."). If there is any external means of measuring the worth of this or any training, it is in this relative term: "How much has this aided this person to be more effective in their work?"

Although this determination can only be made over the long haul, the work in Applications provides valuable assistance to the individual in coalescing the accumulated mass of material from all of his classes into a single coherent organic body of dynamic interactive craft that he can then develop at his own pace throughout his creative career.

FINAL NOTE

I have made several omissions in the program during the period of Application and I wish to make note of them because they are fairly important.

First, there is the matter of the musical cues tape. I generally use (and recommend use of) at least three tapes during this period. These tapes work best in this section when the actors are instructed to react to the tape in essence (and, of course, nonverbally) as their character would. This can be done using one area of essence work to focus the exploration (emotions, intentions, energy, and so forth), or the instruction could be worded in such a way as to leave the exploration open-ended in terms of focus. Either way, by responding as their character would respond, actors often make unusual and valuable discoveries about their characters, while at the same time gaining a new perspective on the work as a whole. This can be a very valuable experience and I would be remiss not to mention it here.

Another valuable tool I have not yet mentioned is the class project. Although I have had classes that did not have the necessary creative energy or initiative to pursue this area of study, in those classes that have, I found it to be very rewarding in many ways. I have indexed some of the more valuable projects in Appendix IV, and so I will not discuss them at length here. I will say that in the more useful and exciting projects, students have prepared (in and outside class time) for up to six months, applying independently the principles learned in my (and my team teachers') classes, to achieve some highly inspiring creative results that were worthy of production.

6
PRACTICAL APPLICATIONS

NOTES FROM A FORMER STUDENT: DAVID HODGE

This brief chapter is designed to show how I applied the theory and training I received from Jean Sabatine in movement for the actor to the practical problems I encountered in three disparate characterizations.

I will explain how this movement theory aided my understanding and performance of Paris in *The Golden Apple*, Scapino in *Scapino!*, and Teddy in *When You Comin' Back Red Ryder?* These three examples have not been arranged chronologically, although they were all performed in 1976.

All three roles were performed at the Pennsylvania State University where I received my Master of Fine Arts degree (MFA) in Acting in 1977. *The Golden Apple* was one of the productions of the 1976 Festival of American Theatre, the professional summer stock series produced by Pennsylvania State. *Scapino!* served as the show and role that focused my monograph in the fall of 1976. *When You Comin' Back Red Ryder?* was performed in the spring of 1976. I chose this order to more clearly reveal how I used this movement theory in the three major approaches that can be taken to character development. In *The Golden Apple* I used an external approach. In *Scapino!* I used a combination of external and internal approaches. For *When You Comin' Back Red Ryder?* I used an internal method primarily.

Partly because *The Golden Apple* is a musical comedy (and therefore, not meant to have much depth), and partly because of the nature of this particular script (which is based on the story of Helen of Troy, but set in Washington state in the post Spanish-American War era), the only approach I could use with Paris was an external one.

Paris is an all-dance mime role. In our early work Jean and I concentrated on the dance sequences hoping to learn as much about the character as possible. We discovered very early on that as a successful traveling salesman, Paris must have a great deal of charm, assuredness, and sex appeal. Since he communicates everything through his movement, he must have grace and style. Also, his movements must be crystal clear in intent and execution. It was a *very* tall order I thought, and a little intimidating at first. All I could do was to begin at the beginning and hope my training and abilities would prevail.

In learning the dance and setting some early business in the mime sequences I realized I was merely executing the idea of the movements and not filling them with the meaning and the character, so I set about the task of finding the essence of Paris.

His physical essence was, of course, upright, cocky, and fluid. This essence study looked something like this: His raised eyebrow and half-embarrassed smile fit best atop a jaunty torso on a head proudly wagging from side to side, bouncing along with the natural swing provided by an almost ridiculously springy step.

As I searched the final form of this rough draft of Paris' physical essence, I began to suspect that I could not only use the essence literally in the performance, but I was also simultaneously opening the doors to the next essence study—the energy essence.

I found Paris' energy to be a constant flow of positively charged ions humming cheerily along corridors of knowing wonder. The image that I finally used to guide my exploration was that of a balloon that has been blown up to capacity and then released without tying off the end. The only differences being that this balloon never ran out of air, made a graceful whooshing sound, and artful swirls and daring dips for constantly appreciative and loving audiences.

From these studies I learned, in the earliest and most pleasant ways, the level of reality Paris lives in: His luck is incredible and it always has been. He is so used to having it he would be nonchalant about his own good fortune were it not for his amusement at himself for enjoying that fact so entirely. It is a natural (and slightly embarrassing) fact that women swoon at the sight of him. Paris has so much luck and natural talent that he really needs no more intellectual prowess than a poker player who is continually dealt the same royal straight flush.

SCAPINO

Scapino! (The Frank Dunlop/Jim Dale version of Moliere's *Les Fourber-ries de Scapin)* is a unique script. Moliere's original script and characters were modeled on the Commedia dell' Arte. Dunlop and Dale tried (I believe successfully) to remain true to the major intentions of Moliere and the fun-loving spirit of the Commedia he copied. They updated the characters and dialogue to include all the local color and contemporary references that were such a part of the Commedia, while keeping the sense or suggestion of improvisation so essential to the form.

To help me in my task I eventually used every resource I possess, including endurance. Of course, I used standard script and character analysis. The following is an excerpt from my journal for this production:

FRIDAY, SEPTEMBER 17

... action revolves around Scapino. He is the innovator. As the play progresses he assumes a more and more active role in the occurrences. His performance has the quality of an ever-increasing metronome that reaches its climax in the bag scene. Just as important, however, and also ruled by the metronome effect, is the personal rapport Scapino has with the audience. By the end of the first act, each audience member must feel a close friendship with Scapino. By the end of the play, the entire audience must be his unalterable ally. Laughter isn't enough for him (me), he (I) must be magnetic, innocently-worldly, intelligent, witty, benign, wise, child-like, and generally loveable.

Scapino is on top of every situation. He is cool. He is an operator. If there is a "No!" to any question, he can change it to a "Yes!" He refuses to accept any fact as unalterable, because it is probably a fabrication of the mind of a man. And most men are weak. To change the fact, therefore, all he has to do is to change the man's mind.

This intellectualization was part of the external portion of my work on *Scapino!* More important than this external understanding was knowledge I gained from the essence studies we were all assigned:

SUNDAY, SEPTEMBER 19

My essence studies have been quite rewarding. I have done all the assigned essences. My (Scapino's) physical essence is a controlled self-amused cockiness (which was a carryover from Paris in *The Golden Apple*). A civilized, controlled vibrating zest for life hums cheerily along his entire frame (and through each movement) in exquisite harmony with itself. All his parts (physical, emotional, and intellectual) are honed with immaculate precision into an interlocking network of joyous unity.

My energy essence was actually a furthering of the physical theme. As Scapino approaches life in his erect, self-assured, physical manner, an entire continent of stored energy fills him with a vast potential for action, but action as directed by his mind. Every action is controlled by his mind. He controls the amount and direction and kind of energy used for a certain activity. It is metered, measured, and ordered. But he is not a creature of the mind alone: He depends a great deal on his instinct and inspiration to guide his mind. These open patterns of thought reveal courses of possible action spontaneously and inexplicably. He can afford to be cocky with this kind of creative power backing him up.

He loves to place himself in positions that present great challenge and as all such situations present him with great potential for amusement, they provide him with the most enjoyable contact with the world. He is the Bobby Fisher of the game of life.

My exterior animal is an affectionate, wide-eyed, innocent, and guileless giraffe. Very controlled, very premeditated movement, constrained by his physical dissimilarity, almost aloof, but compassionate and understanding. He is not lonely, but he is alone.

My interior animal is an otter. Joyous, charming, fearlessly affable, agile, and quick-witted, he is everyone's friend. (And yet, because no one can keep up with this indefatigable character, he can never form a total bond with anyone. And as women tend to slow one down, he avoids "entanglements," although he has sex often in the same happy spirit as anything else he gets into.) He is sleek, smooth, strong, and in his own disarming, charming, harmless way, aggressive. Without fear or peer, he is king of the world which he need not own. Not only is ownership pedestrian and beneath him, it would also bore him witless and he knows it!

SUNDAY, SEPTEMBER 19

The performance of these studies before the entire cast (which Jean [Sabatine] as Movement Director required of all the cast), revealed in better detail and more fully than any discussion could, each character's comedic potential. Also apparent was the true nature of characters' relationships and theatrical purpose.

Through occasional group improvisatioins based on these essence studies the cast reestablished contact with the self-evident truth that the comedy in *Scapino!* is dependent, in large measure, on the contrasting character types and their skillful interaction. Although I always had believed that comedy is essentially a relationship (which is humorous), I had never had such a practical demonstration of that fact before this.

TEDDY

The most elaborate and successful use to which I have put my movement training was with Teddy in Mark Medoff's *When You Comin' Back Red Ryder?* Due to the nature of Teddy I decided to use an internal approach primarily. Although it possesses some humorous moments, *When You Comin Back Red Ryder?* is not a comedy. I was most concerned, therefore, with building the reality of a character who some have variously called disturbed, deranged, and psychotic.

Once again I began with script and character analysis. The following are taken from my journal for Teddy:

I have come to the concusion that Teddy is so complex that I have had to break down his actions into Roles, and Schizoid personalities. Within any one personality he is capable of a broad range of roles, although in some he is naturally Roleless—truly genuine.

At the same time, however, I realized that this cerebral breakdown was only meant to act as a signpost for a traveler moving too fast on an expressway to reason these things out. Those transitions I knew must become almost mechanical, and the personalities of each a full-blown reality within my own organic reality.

I realized too that the Super-Objective, or more accurately the Super-Reality, must not operate independently of the detours of this Schizoid personality, but rather act as the unifying and driving force behind their existence. In other words, there is a spine to Teddy that keeps him true to some goal in all his roles and personalities.

MARCH 7 (CONTINUED)

There is one dominant personality—the omniscient, unmoved, implaca-ble, unaffected, dissociated Teddy who has no passion—only clinical perception of self in relation to the world. A truly honest—"Mr. Spock-gone-one-step-beyond"—Watcher. This personality too has only one level of existence and is not a "Role." [Later I would refer to his personality as "Big Nurse" from *One Flew Over the Cuckoo's Nest*]

I realized also that the humanity of the man is missing if I contented myself with saying, "He's crazy." I had to know how and why.

MARCH 7 (CONTINUED)

Teddy is a tortured soul, who can find no satisfaction in anything he does. There is no home base for him, no safety. He is driven from inaction by his realization that that is an action (cowardly and prone to disaster), while he also realizes that this is a flight from the responsibility of one's action. He thus aggressively assumes the mantle of action as a tool, a conscious effort toward finding, seeking, achieving the goal that he sees as simultaneously falacious, unreachable, nonexistent, and the only noble or worthwhile desire worthy of any effort. All the while he hates and despises nobility as illusion, he also desperately loves and embraces true nobility as real, and being the *only* worthwhile reality in an otherwise empty existence.

His Watcher knows all this in him and the world, and yet is incapable of resolving his dilemma for him. (The only capability it has is to keep him from losing sight of his unseen destination. It can only control the personalities to prevent one from dominating the others.)

The substance of Teddy's character was something that I could achieve only by identifying with him. I had no trouble in constructing this gut portion of his personality, however.

FEBRUARY 7

I must find those incidents that turned his genius more to madness. I can identify some very personally right off the bat—mid-sixties creative surge of the young, intellectuals, liberals (a revolution out of "The Age of Apathy" perhaps), Kennedy's assassination, the right-wing backlash against them, and finally militant blacks, the ghetto rebellions, and Vietnam. And (herein lies the major key) the return of the disillusioned veteran of the war to a hostile and ravaged America ... Who accepted him? Who loved him? Who cared for and protected him? Not his peer group—totally unable to relate to this fanatically intense young breed. Not the establishment or the older set who, also alienated from him, distrusted and feared him. Not even his family who no longer knew him. He was alone—with his nightmares—and hated for them ... He was the killer loose in the herd, and they hated him because they feared him ... And when he could find no kindred spirits—his reaction could be: Teddy's ...

The leap from all that knowledge (or speculation) to its reality seemed impossible. Then I began a series of independent movement improvisations that began to open up the organic connection to Teddy.

I started with a physical essence study of Teddy. The result was a superbly muscled and coordinated body filled with tension, moving in spasms of finely honed precision toward the achievement of immediate goals. There was no wasted emotion, no artful swirls, no laziness, no hesitancy. From a position of seeming rest would spring sudden precise gestures that could stop at the conclusion or at any point along its path—clearly, as though the movement had been intended to be executed just that way.

I evolved several useful images to help me find Teddy's physical essence: an attacking rattlesnake, a cold-blooded gunslinger, an inscrutable Samurai warrior facing incredible odds.

My energy essence turned out to be (not very surprisingly) a superbly controlled current vibrating invisibly, powerfully within a granite statue encompassed in a fine shell of platinum. The study looked rather like a karate exhibition—with all the concentration, intense focus, and sudden whiplike movements contained in karate—but the movements weren't classical karate moves. Also the speed changed rapidly from a seeming full stop to as fast as I could move to slow motion, and all through the spectrum I could imagine and manage.

I next tried an intention study and found that Teddy's intentions are pure, powerful, and intense and they change suddenly and inscrutably without visible transition. The intensity never diminishes—even when his intention is to listen, taste, divine, or observe, his concentration is pure, his area of focus frighteningly finite.

I began to understand Teddy as a thinker and a doer—that is, I knew *what* and *how* he thinks and acts—but I still could not understand *why.*

I next attempted an emotional study, but got nowhere. I could think of nothing, and nothing would come. The sudden transitions continued to be premeditated and illusive. The only thing I learned from this was that I would need something more than just myself to help me find the emotional Teddy.

I began to ponder what else I could do to help me make the final leap into Teddy. Suddenly I realized that my approach to date had been too calculated (and too logical). My studies had all been goal-oriented to some degree, and now this last goal loomed so large before me I could not ignore its presence, even while I was doing my explorations!

Finally, I decided on a movement tape for Teddy. I respond well to music and felt that it was bound to reveal something to me. No one else could make a tape for me, and since I had the proper equipment and had made several before (for Jean Sabatine's movement course), I set out to find "Teddy music." Once accumulated, I tried to mindlessly throw myself into the project.

I tried not to censor or edit the material in any conscious way other than to place different visceral or emotional qualities in close proximity to each other. I used what in film would be called a cross-fade technique. Sometimes I allowed one piece of music to play under another contrasting piece, and sometimes I played two pieces at the same volume. I used some of the material several times with different types of transitions into and out of a certain piece of music.

I did not listen to any of the tape once I had recorded it, and I consciously avoided planning the tape. When I felt that this or that piece of music had gone on long enough, I found another that seemed to affect my state of mind radically. When I was finished, I had a tape almost thirty minutes long composed of selections by over a dozen different artists.

I waited two days before I even thought about it again, and attempted to carry on with other rehearsal work. I believe that my subconscious was busy digesting the experience of the single three-hour taping session (for my work became somehow translucently different), but I avoided conscious deliberation of it.

I set up my tape recorder and speakers in the downstairs Pavilion (a dance studio) an hour-and-a-half before rehearsal on March 17th. I carried a lamp that gave off a warm and gentle light into the studio. I then did an easy physical warmup, followed by a thorough relaxation exercise. When I felt free from tension, I turned on the tape and relaxed back to the floor with a sense of mild euphoric anxiety, knowing that I was ready to follow wherever the music took me.

When the music was over, I lay down in a pool of sweat, utterly free of tension, my mind filled with images and memories I could have only formed in a dream-state. The juxtaposition of types of music (such as the soul-rending "Lowland Lullaby" from Yusef Lateef's album *The Gentle Giant*, and the vicious rock 'em, sock 'em "Non-Stop Home" from the Weather Report album *Mysterious Traveller)* opened up the organic connection in me that had eluded me until then.

FEBRUARY 12

For example: At one point in the tape there was a piece of music ("One of These Days" from Pink Floyd's album *Meddle)* that inspired me to run in a huge circle around the perimeters of the room. At first it was just running for the sake of running, because it felt good. Then it suddenly seemed as though I were pursuing something. As I ran that thing changed into different images I had desired in my youth: a catcher's mitt, a watch, to play third base, to make the winning touchdown, to have people cheer for me. The progression led me farther into that part of myself that is insecure, and as that happened the images became more abstract: to be loved by everyone, to be respected by everyone, to be intelligent, to be wise, to transcend wanting. But the farther I ran and the harder I tried the farther out of reach those things seemed. And as I realized that, the fear seemed to creep up on me from behind—as though as fast as I was running the treadmill was carrying me faster still in the opposite direction—toward failure, degradation, humiliation. Images came to mind, and it seemed I had to run faster to escape from each one—Soon, I realized I was running from fear more than desire, but I couldn't stop. I had to keep going but with each loop around the room I felt more tired, and with the fatigue came a profound hopelessness—an awareness of the futility of my action, finally the stupidity of my efforts came to me like a blinding light and stopped me dead in my tracks. As I stood there gasping for air, and watching my sweat fall onto the floor, Yusef Lateef's *Lowland Lullaby* came on again and I saw all my own private hopes and dreams as a kind of three-dimensional structure. The dimensions consisted of simultaneous sensations of emotion, abstract ideas, and physical imagery. They stood briefly outlined against a desolate background that made no sense—until it rushed upon me (in the unreal timelessness of a dream where occurrences are both extremely fast and slow). The background were all the sights and sounds, odors, thoughts, and feelings of which I am ashamed and afraid. And as they came at me the Beautiful tower of dreams turned to ash and collapsed in upon itself.

I writhed in a massive seizure—convulsed in upon myself crying out, and in that lost and desperate moment found all the anger at myself and, still in pain, cried in rage—straightening and lifting, my arms flailed at the air for a few moments until all my energy was gone and I was empty. I sagged into myself, onto my knees and cried as I remembered scene after scene from my past that moved me to tears.

The next moment, when the next violent piece of music began, the juxtaposition of the selections stopped me from crying, sobering me almost like the drunk who's been slapped in the face by his outraged wife, and I straightened proudly—defensively—looking around to see if anyone had seen me. (Through this entire process I never lost track of the awareness that I was doing an exercise. It was as though someone had given me permission to probe my psyche as though it belonged to someone else. In a sense it did. I knew that there were memories that wouldn't fit the tape, and that the tape was not engineered to reveal me, but Teddy—or at least the Teddy within me. I was allowing the tape to restructure my experience to show me the reaction this new structure would have on me. In this way, while reacting honestly, I never "freaked out" or even worried about that possibility. I was empathizing—as though I had direct mind contact with a friend in pain. I was safe, Teddy was in trouble.)

It seemed perfectly natural that, filled with so much vital pain and his dynamic will to overcome the world (and himself), this man could feel simultaneous and conflicting emotions of such magnitude that he could satisfy his need to express both only by committing himself totally to one at a time—that his action in doing so would be flavored by the other emotion—and that his transition from the one to the other would be instantaneous, violent, and *seem* to be incomprehensible. I realized the nature of Teddy's dilemma and his precarious balance on the razor's edge of insanity.

It was as though each of his many personalities were alive, writhing in pain just below his iron-fisted will, crying for the opportunity for expression—only coming to the surface when the proper obscure button was pushed within me.

It is important to remember that *only at this point* did I achieve an organic knowledge of the inner nature of Teddy. The next step in this creative chain was the most important, however. I had to carry this awareness onto the stage and make it work for me there, or all the work was useless.

I managed to do this very easily through an elaborate discipline that I subjected myself to every night. During the final run throughs, dress rehearsals, and through the run of the show, my activities were planned very carefully.

At 5:00 P.M. I went to room 119 in the Arts Building for a warmup and dance rehearsal with Jazz Dance Theatre. (This was an excellent physical and mental exercise that I used as part of my preparation. The dancing was channeled into Teddy's physical self-challenge and my mind flew freely into exploration of the joyous and physical Teddy while my body was being tuned to "perfect control.")

At 7:00 P.M. I walked (or ran) to the Pavilion and, while exchanging pleasantries with the cast and crew, proceeded to the next level of preparation. This involved getting into costume and make-up, and setting up my tape recorder and headphones with the improvisation tape on it.

A very important and crucial step came just before I put on the headphones. This was the physical action of loading the revolver used to shoot one of the characters at the close of Act One.

At 7:45 P.M. I put on the headphones and started the tape. Each night, I timed the tape's conclusion with my entrance—twenty minutes into Act One.

When I was called for places (about five minutes before my entrance), I went up with Debbie Studor (who played Teddy's girlfriend, Cheryl) to the off-stage waiting area, picked up the gun, and put it beside me while I proceeded to do between 50 and 75 sit-ups, and 15 to 35 push-ups which I finished just prior to my entrance!

I found this preparation to be of invaluable aid because it produced for me the physical state that was necessary (Teddy and his girlfriend had supposedly pushed a V.W. van a mile-and-a-half to the gas station), and the mental state that I had found from the improvisation tape. It was effortless to walk on stage in the proper condition both physically and mentally because the acting was merely a release of the past three hours of organic preparation.

I am not trying to claim that the interpretations I have given to these characters are invariably and inviolably correct. That would be foolish. Each actor brings a different set of strengths, weaknesses, and experiences to a given role. Indeed one of my major strengths as an actor is that I have a tremendous reserve of energy. A close inspection of the three roles I have described—especially the energy essences—will reveal my consistent use of that strength. Another actor's approach to these same characters and the results he achieves will differ from mine and could still be valid. Add to these facts the further complications of the extreme variance in directional approach, temperament, and casting possibilities, and it is easy to see that a quite different, equally plausible, interpretation of each role I described might develop.

I have tried to show how Jean Sabatine's movement training (specifically her *essence* theory) has aided me in my development of three radically different characterizations. I have tried to show that these *Explorations* can be effectively applied to any role or production. The only rules are: use what helps, change or restructure the basic explorations to suit your needs, don't be afraid of or disheartened by failure, and keep an open mind.

I now feel confident in my ability to competently approach a wide range of theatrical experiences. I am not bound by preconceived ideas of what is needed in developing a characterization—I can put on the mask and find out from it what lies behind it (as I did with Paris), I can dig into the character's guts and find the mask he wears (as I did with Teddy), or I can use both approaches simultaneously (as I did with Scapino). I do have an ultimate goal in all my acting, however, regardless of the approach to characterization, and that is to commit myself so fully to the creation in rehearsal and to preparation on the night of performance that I do not need to consciously monitor my performance on stage.

My experiences with Teddy in *When You Comin' Back Red Ryder?* confirmed my belief in the viability of a performance without conscious control. To achieve this goal I try to maintain an attitude of noninterference. Once the director and I have done all that can be done in the manner of preparation, I endeavor to merely let the performance happen. In this way I seek to free myself from my mind's conscious tampering with the more reliable organic process. This is a process of *action without self-awareness.*

I found this movement training geared perfectly to teaching me the techniques and discipline necessary to effect this type of performance. Step by step, using the method shown in this book, I was led closer and closer toward independence. This training, intelligently combined with competent acting training, has given me a viable craft that I continue to develop and adapt as the need and opportunity arises.

Since graduation from Penn State I have worked in regional theatre as a member of Actor's Equity Association and in T.V. and film as a member of the Screen Actor's Guild, and the tools I learned in my movement training are still with me. I may not need to do an entire series of essence studies for every role, but I often choose one or two to help me in areas with which I feel I am having difficulty. And even when I do not literally prepare a study, just the many specific ways I now have of focusing on a particular problem is an aid to its solution.

7
CONCLUSION

The obvious focus of this book is the effort to communicate what I feel to be important theories and training methods to teachers, and future teachers, of movement. A second, and perhaps more important focus, is the attempt to awaken in the theatre profession as a whole (especially actors, directors, students, teachers, and related specialists) the need for a better understanding and appreciation of good movement training for actors.

My hope, beyond these two considerations, is that all theatre specialists and generalists who read this book will be able to use some of the exercises, explorations, applications, and principles set forth here in their own work. Specialists should find they can easily incorporate them into their own existing frame of reference, and adapt the principles to special problems encountered in production. Generalists should find useful unifying principles so necessary to them. Teachers of all performing disciplines (especially acting teachers) should find value in many areas of the book. This, at least, is my hope.

What I know to be true is that this method and these theories have worked for me and for my students. I know that the mind/body connection is the organic reality of human existence and that awareness and control of this reality is essential for an actor. And I know that each person must take responsibility for building their own discipline and system of thought. Thus, I also know and desire that each person will take what is useful to them and make it uniquely their own.

Thousands of years ago the Greeks lived by the espoused belief that the mind and body must be developed equally to achieve a balance in the being. Their theatre, at its height, was a dynamic example of and tribute to that principle. It is perhaps ironic that I find myself in a position of defending this principle in today's flourishing theatrical age. Perhaps the terminology or the manner of training, or even the application of the theory is new, but the truth about the human condition has not changed.

If it is true that the mind and the body are mutually effecting parts of a single organic entity, can we, as theatre artists, afford the luxury of ignoring that fact, regardless of our specialization? And can we, as responsible professionals, content ourselves with our own awareness of this important fact without caring about the communication of our awareness and its uses to new or developing talents not yet so aware? Obviously, we cannot do either and continue to believe we are sincere in our desire to perfect our art form.

Here then is one small part of my continuing effort to communicate my hard-won understanding of this most important reality. Here is the use to which I have put this fact. And here is my hope that at least some of you will find this work beneficial to your own.

APPENDIXES

APPENDIX 1: ONE YEAR'S WORK
(IN SYLLABUS FORMAT)

Let us assume we are dealing with a college classroom situation in which each class is one-and-a-half hours in length, each week there are three class sessions (say Monday, Wednesday, and Friday), and in this semester system there are fifteen weeks to the term. This means that the movement course will either cover one semester (half a school year) or two semesters (a full school year).

The ideal course for serious professionally oriented students would be one year's study. This is the only way all the material can be thoroughly presented and dealt with by the actor. Also, students need at least one year to even hope to maximize the potential of the work. In an introductory course with general college or even general drama students, a survey of the material provided in a single semester can be surprisingly effective and stimulating. Selectivity then becomes the key to constructing the course design. Let's concentrate on the ideal, however, because this allows us to examine the design in greater detail and, even in beginning students, is the *most* effective way to proceed.

Generally, in the first semester I direct almost all the theory and effort toward the actor, then in the second semester the focus changes to characterization, and finally, to scene work. The reasons for this are obvious, but deserve brief discussion:

1. The actor must always start with himself.
   a. The actor's only permanent tools are his body, voice, experience, intelligence, sensitivity, and creativity.
   b. The actor's tools must be disciplined, organized, and conditioned before he is ready to employ them meaningfully.
   c. It is important for the actor to understand, in a very immediate and personal sense, how these principles operate before he can hope to apply them to characterization.

2. Before the relationship of one character to another can be understood, each actor must understand his relationship to his character.
   a. An actor must first understand his character before he can hope to understand how and why his character relates to another.
   b. By applying the personalization tools first to the character, the actor draws on personal experience to build a past for his character so that the character's present has justification.
   c. Through the accumulated understanding of (and empathy with) the character, the actor builds a solid foundation for the scene work.

3. Work on a scene should never be imposed from preconceptions unsupported by practical understandings of the character's make-up and motivations.
   a. Scenes are complicated interactions and can easily lead to an intellectual morass.
   b. Once both actors in a scene are in command of their character, the scene can naturally evolve from the dynamic interaction of the three-dimensional persons commanded by the actors.
   c. Characters with an organic reality are essential to this kind of scene work, so unless an actor has first been trained to understand and work organically, scene work can be an exercise in futility.

Here then is the general outline of one year's work in this basic, organically-oriented movement class. Keep in mind that it is only a model, and is in practice very, very flexible. At the same time remember that while time frames within the sequence of sections may be altered (depending on the needs and capacities of the class), the general design is the one I have found most suited to the task at hand, and any significant decision to change the order of progression from one sequence to the next should first be carefully considered.

MOVEMENT COURSE FOR ACTORS (A FIRST SEMESTER)

Objective—Establishment of the Organic Connection

My objective in the physical training of the actor is the integration of the mind and body: The whole organism in harmony with itself so that it is ready for interaction. This is the natural organic connection.

I start by bringing the actor to a neutral state, ridding him of personal mannerisms. If an actor stuck to a particular movement pattern, he would become incapable of portraying any other character, and he would be type casting himself. He limits himself rather than helping to expand his range by not being able to experience and empathize with all physical movements, attitudes, and emotions.

Effective training of the actor can only begin when he is open to new ideas and can unleash the body and mind of harmful physical and emotional problems.

Goal One

Help the actor to find the proper balance of tension and relaxation to bring the body to a ready state. The actor must find the proper balance between these two elements. This enables the flow of energy to go in and out of the body, rather than getting blocked inside—to feel alive, which most of all enables the actor to react. Even when just standing on stage an actor should be full of inner life (internal energy).

One of the main problems is excessive tension that cuts off the flow of energy, limiting the actor's physical movement as well as his expression (inner life). The actor needs to work to find the proper balance of tension and relaxation to keep the body and mind ready for action.

Goal Two

Help the actor to establish proper breathing habits in relationship to his movement. Improper breathing patterns increase unnecessary tension and decrease the mind's and body's ability to act and react freely to internal and external stimulus.

The work spent harmonizing breathing with movement patterns harmonizes with and complements the efforts expended in voice and speech classes, and aids in establishing the positive flow of energy for both speech and movement.

Goal Three

Assist the actor in finding and maintaining his own natural alignment and in developing his awareness of the related concept of center. An actor who can control his body attitude so that he can sense and maintain his own natural alignment is well on the way to mastering the ability to center himself physically and emotionally. This also is helpful in eliminating radical personal physical mannerisms and masses of unnecessary tensions, which impede development of proper breathing habits and efficient flow of energy.

Goal Four

A carefully arranged series of physical exercises and explorations helps to reveal the natural interactive relationship of the mind and body. An actor solely dependent on his intellect closes himself off to his natural organic reality, whereas one totally focused on his body is less capable of making intelligent choices.

Syllabus: Movement for Actors
(First Semester)

I. *Daily Class Routine*
   A. Tension/Relaxation
   B. Exercises/Technique
   C. Explorations
   D. Applications
   E. Discussion

II. *Course Content*
   A. Explores basic concepts in movement
      1. Explores basic concepts of Space, Time, Energy
      2. Explores parameters of human movement, that is, Body explorations
      3. Explores Body/Mind relationship, that is, Internal/External
      4. Explores individual/world relationship through movement
   B. Subjects Covered
      1. Alignment/breath
      2. Body explorations
      3. Walking/posture (what this tells us about individuals)
      4. Space (what it is/how to use it [direction, levels, range, design, focus])
      5. Gesture (social/functional)
      6. Essence theory of movement/abstraction theory
      7. Energy (percussive, sustained, swinging, vibratory, suspend, collapse)
      8. Action verbs
      9. Time
     10. Animal Essences (internal/external)
     11. Fragment (follow through)

    C. Projects (involving outside class time)
        1. Two walk studies (their own and another's)
        2. Two gesture studies (functional and social)
        3. Haiku abstraction
        4. Energy study of themselves
        5. Action verb essence study
        6. Line essence study
        7. Animal essence study
        8. Physical essence study (space, time, energy)
        9. Two short papers on movement of character in a play
      10. One class project on any area covered

III. *Course Breakdown*
    A. First and second weeks
        1. Tension/relaxation
        2. Alignment and breath
        3. Teaching exercises
        4. Body exploration
    B. Third week (*Class Routine)*
        1. Shortened period of
            a. tension/relaxation
            b. alignment and breath
            c. exercises
        2. Body explorations
        3. Walks
    C. Fourth and fifth weeks
        1. Return to *class routine*
        2. Space chapter
        3. First movement tape
        4. Folk dance
    D. Sixth week
        1. Class routine
        2. Essence theory
        3. Gestures
            a. Social
            b. Functional
    E. Seventh week
        1. Class routine
        2. Haiku essence (essence of meaning)
        3. Energy study
        4. First paper due
    F. Eighth week
        1. Class routine
        2. Energy essence
        3. Action verbs
        4. Energy tape
    G. Ninth and tenth weeks
        1. Class routine

2. Action verb study
3. Line essence
4. Line essence study
H. Eleventh week
  1. Class routine
  2. Animal essence
  3. Animal essence study
I. Twelfth and thirteenth weeks
  1. Class routine
  2. Time (tempo, duration, rhythm pattern, accent, counterpoint)
  3. Exploration of above elements
  4. Time tape
  5. Rhythm essence
  6. Second paper due
J. Fourteenth week
  1. Class routine
  2. Physical essence of self (space, time, energy)
K. Fifteenth week
  1. Presentation of Final Project (student's choice)
  2. Presentation of Class Project (as it stands)
  3. Discussion of Relation of Past to Future Work

A MOVEMENT COURSE FOR ACTORS (SECOND SEMESTER)

This semester focuses on physicalization of a character and movement in a scene.

Objective

Reinforce and extend organic connection to include characterization. If it is true that the actor as a human being has a natural organic connection, it is also true that any character he will be asked to play will also have a mind/body relationship organic to him. This phase of study focuses in on assisting the actor to find through his by now sensitive instrument, the organic reality of his character.

Goal One

Maintain and further develop all the positive elements the actor has learned in the preceding semester (that is, proper tension/relaxation, breathing, alignment, and so on).

213

Goal Two

Establish the understanding that manipulation of internal (memory, emotions, attitudes, and so on) and external (bodily positions, altering center, and alignment movements, space, time, energy, and so on) elements aids in the creation of a new sense of self—that is, characterization.

Goal Three

Develop and control specific characterizations through the manipulation of the elements previously covered, using sophisticated extensions of techniques already learned.

Syllabus: Movement for Actors
(Second Semester)

Class Structure
1. Warmup Exercises
2. Explorations
3. Applications
4. Discussion

I. *Material Covered*
   To review the major elements covered in last semester's work.
   1. Basic elements of movement
      A. Space
      B. Time
      C. Energy
   2. Elements of tension—relaxation—alignment
   3. Essence theory
      A. Line
      B. Action verb
      C. Gesture

II. *Physicalization of a Character (inner—outer) Through Essence Work**
   1. Walk
   2. Posture—Center
   3. Mannerisms
   4. Moods—emotions
   5. Interest
   6. Wants—needs
   7. Etc. (Who—What—Where—Why)

III. *An Understanding of His/Her Inner and Outer Being*
   1. Use of space
   2. Energy

*Actors will select a scene from a contemporary play, choosing characters that are close to themselves in age.

3. Rhythm essence (internal conflicts)
4. Animal studies (inner—outer essence of character)
5. Emotional make-up of the character

IV. *Movement in the Scene*
1. Energy essence of the scene
2. Counterpoint (Yin-Yang) of scene
3. Animal essences together with scene
4. Major intention of the scene
5. Emotional thread
6. Line essence work extended

V. *Additional Work*
1. Movement tapes
2. Projects
3. Other problems we find during our work

APPENDIX 2:
SAMPLE CLASS STRUCTURES

Because of the changing nature of the material, the make-up of class-room activity, and breakdown of class time into various activities will change according to the needs of the material. For instance, my first classes are usually devoted almost entirely to teaching exercises and working on alignment, breathing techniques, and relaxation/tension problems. Later classes, while using these techniques in an approximately thirty minute warmup, will be devoted to body or movement explorations, while even later classes will be broken down into perhaps three separate portions of Warmup, Exploration, and Presentation or Application. Some classes will involve a single warmup and the rest of the time will be devoted to students working together (under my supervision, if not guidance) on the class project (see Appendix 3).

I have outlined two sample class structures: one from the first semester and one from the second semester. Notice that the outline of the first semester class involves an exploration of energy and a presentation of Haiku Essence studies introduced and assigned from a previous class. This is a useful tool to demonstrate similarities between seemingly unrelated topics and provides the sensation and awareness of organic growth for students. Please notice also the increased number and sophistication of exercises in the second semester. Arm patterns are added by this time, as well as the more difficult balancing exercises.

Finally, the basic diifference between the two classes is that, although both involve the concept of energy, the first semester class deals with energy as it affects and applies to the actor, and in the second semester, those same concepts are used by the actor in relationship to the character.

Sample Class Structure
(First Semester)

Remember we are using a one-and-a-half hour class period as the model. This is a session seven weeks into the fifteen-week term. The class will be divided roughly into thirds:

1. Exercises and warmup session (25 to 35 minutes)
2. Explorations (20 to 30 minutes)
3. Presentation (20 to 30 minutes)
4. Discussion (5 to 10 minutes)

I. Exercises
The usual sequence for developmental warmup on a typical day:

1. Basics

    Relaxation
    Breathing and Spine work
    Posture Alignment
    Spine Studies

2. Isolations

    Head, Shoulders, Rib Cage, Pelvis

3. General Exercises

    Stretch and Swing
    Stretch to Side
    Pliés (demi and grand)
    Side Stretches
    Leg Extensions
    Parallel Pliés
    Brushes
    Four-Count Stretch

4. Floor Exercises

    Head and Spine
    Up Over the Back, Shoulder Stand Press
    Sequential Sitting Up
    Knee into Chest
    Pushups (men, 15; women, 10)
    Flex and Extend
    Second Position Flex and Stretch
    Bounce, Bounce, and Up

5. Ending the Warmup

    Foot Flexibility
    Jumps
    Frustration Jumps
    Breath Rhythm

II. Explorations
Energy:*
a. energy and pure movement
b. energy and gesture
III. Presentation
Haiku studies
IV. Discussion
Relate Haikus to Energy

Sample Class Structure
(Second Semester)

Again, we are using a one-and-a-half hour class period. This is perhaps seven weeks into a fifteen-week term. The class is divided again into thirds:

1. Exercises (30 minutes)
2. Exploration (20 minutes)
3. Application and Discussion (40 minutes)

I. Exercises
1. Spine Studies
Breathing in
Swing and Up
2. Isolations
Head Rotation
Head Percussive
Rib Cage
Pelvis (Sustained Circling)
Percussive Pelvic
Shoulder Roll
3. General Exercises
Stretch and Swing
Stretch to Side
Plié Sequence
Side Stretches
Leg Extensions
Brushes
Four-Count Stretch

*In the warmup, lead into the Exploration on energy by focusing on energy qualities in the individual exercises. Pliés, for example, can be executed with an awareness of the sustained energy quality they require.

217

Stretch, Side Flat, Side, Back
Layouts

4. Floor Exercises

Up Over the Back
Constructive Rest
Up Over Each Other's Back
Sequential Sitting Up
Pushups (men, 25 to 30; women, 15)
Head and Spine
Leg Up and Stretch
Knees into Chest
Flex and Extend
Second Position Flex and Stretch
Breathe on Hands and Knees
Stretch, Sit, Push Through and Sit
Sit, Push, Sit, Roll
Arch and A
Bounce, Bounce, and Up

5. Ending the Warmup

Foot Flexibility
Jumps
Frustration Jumps
Breath Rhythm

II. Exploration

Explore the concept of the character's energy in terms of the internal versus external qualities that may be present. For instance: "Does this character wish to be perceived as being one thing by those around him (that is, swinging quality that is cool, calm, easygoing) but in reality being something far different internally (that is, vibratory quality—nervous, unsure, insecure)?" "Does your character think he is one thing (that is, sustained quality—even tempered, meticulous, disciplined) but in reality he is something totally different (that is, percussive quality—domineering, dogmatic, compulsive)?" This is only another way of trying to discover hidden facets to your understanding of the character, or to reaffirm previous discoveries whether or not they validate this concept of the character being different inside than what he appears, or attempts to appear, outside. Many people are exactly what they seem and/or are what they want us to think they are.

III. Presentation and Discussion

The major portion of this class is set aside for presentation and discussion of each person's energy essence of their character. Depending on class size and the discussion that evolves from ensuing presentations, a second day of presentations may be necessary. This is typical of the problem of setting a firm line for the second semester classes.

Generally warmup sessions are more interesting and energizing when done to music. This is only so if the exercises are known so thoroughly that the music is not a distraction, but serves rather to focus and punctuate the work. Since constant music can also serve as a distraction, careful selection of musical pieces to coordinate with certain series of exercises is the best avenue of approach.

The best type of music to use in this class is music that has a definite ¼ beat, is currently popular, or rather, is performed by musicians recognized and appreciated by students in the class. This provides a relaxing atmosphere and establishes the comforting feeling that "This is something I can relate to," which in turn subliminally translates to the feeling "I can do this," and "I want to do this."

Music that does not provide a relatively easy reference point for the majority of the students in a class lends itself to sponsoring cliquish or elitist attitudes, which translate into competitiveness. If students begin to vie with one another over which movement of Mozart this is or which ballet that comes from—much has been lost compared to the relatively minor gain of having the tempo and count established for you.

Use Common Sense

When choosing music one should always use common sense and personal taste as a guide. Also, although music is a useful tool, it should not become a crutch. Counting verbally, or using a hand drum may be useful alternative methods. Students will many times ask to bring in some of their own music and this is usually a refreshing change of pace in addition to encouraging active participation in the learning process.

Common sense should also be employed in finding the optimum tempo for each exercise. Listen to the music, try the exercise in half-time, normal ¼, and if appropriate, in double-time. Use the tempo of that selection which feels appropriate. If none of the three seems appropriate for that exercise, don't use it. I have seen injuries result from attempting to force an exercise to fit a piece of music not suited to it.

The Right Tempo

For any exercise, however, it is easy to find music in a fairly wide range of tempos that can work to aid the performance of the exercise. So it is not necessary to use inappropriate music. To help set the tempo, I have included in this appendix a table that pairs exercises that can use music as an aid, with a series of suggested musical recordings that can be used in conjunction with each of those exercises.

Since any written guide to the latest popular music would be obsolete before it could get to the presses, I will use a fairly timeless standard of recorded popular music—the Beatles. I rarely use them in my classes anymore, but to help one establish the optimum tempo, they are the most reliable source and reference point. Their place in twentieth-century music is set for the foreseeable future and copies of their records should not be too difficult to secure even in small communities. The records will at least be available through commercial houses for some considerable time to come, unlike some of the lesser known—and probably less historically significant—contemporary recording groups.

Here then is "The Table of Tempos":

TABLE OF TEMPOS

Every exercise with an asterisk (*) preceding it can also be used in conjunction with all of the musical pieces in the Standard Group listing on pp. 226–27, unless otherwise noted.

*BREATHING IN

> Get Back
> Maxwell's Silver Hammer
> Don't Pass Me By
> I Should Have Known Better
> Ballad of John and Yoko
> Honey Don't
> Rock and Roll Music

*SWING AND UP

Note: With the exception of Taxman and What You're Doing, the Standard Group listing is applicable to this exercise.

> Lady Madonna
> Get Back
> Maxwell's Silver Hammer

Glass Onion
Back in the USSR
Eleanor Rigby
Good Day Sunshine
Flying

*HEAD ROTATION (PERCUSSIVE)

Ballad of John and Yoko
Get Back
Maxwell's Silver Hammer
Ob-la-di, Ob-la-da
Flying

*RIB CAGE (PELVIS)

Old Brown Shoe
Get Back
Maxwell's Silver Hammer
Glass Onion
Birthday
Honey Don't
Eleanor Rigby

*SHOULDER ROLL

Old Brown Shoe
Don't Pass Me By
Maxwell's Silver Hammer
Savoy Truffle
Why Don't We Do It in the Road
Honey Don't
Elenor Rigby
Everybody's Trying to be My Baby
Magical Mystery Tour

*STRETCH AND SWING—STRETCH TO SIDE

Get Back
Maxwell's Silver Hammer

Lady Madonna
Eleanor Rigby
Good Day Sunshine

*PLIÉ SEQUENCE PARALLEL—CLASSICAL

Lady Madonna
Paperback Writer
Here Comes the Sun
Dear Prudence
Back in the USSR
Eleanor Rigby
Good Day Sunshine

*SIDE STRETCHES

Two of Us
Maxwell's Silver Hammer
Savoy Truffle
Eleanor Rigby
Good Day Sunshine

*LEG EXTENSIONS

Everybody's Trying to Be My Baby
Two of Us
One After 909
Polythene Pam
Dear Prudence
Ob-la-di, Ob-la-da
Savoy Truffle
Don't Pass Me By

*BRUSHES

What You're Doing
I Should Have Known Better
Good Day Sunshine
Rain
Two of Us

Get Back
Maxwell's Silver Hammer
Back in the USSR
Glass Onion
A Little Help from My Friends
Flying

*FOUR-COUNT STRETCH

Two of Us
Maxwell's Silver Hammer
Here Comes the Sun
Back in the USSR
Ob-la-di, Ob-la-da
Don't Pass Me By
Savoy Truffle
Honey Don't
Eleanor Rigby
Good Day Sunshine
Rock and Roll Music

*STRETCH SIDE, FLAT, SIDE, BACK

Can't Buy Me Love (entire exercise except Step 6 because it is too fast to do this step)
Maxwell's Silver Hammer
Back in the USSR
Savoy Truffle
Ob-la-di, Ob-la-da
Eleanor Rigby
Good Day Sunshine
Lovely Rita
Flying

LAYOUTS

Rain
Get Back
Back in the USSR
Helter Skelter

Cry Baby Cry
Honey Don't
Taxman
Run for Your Life
When I'm Sixty-four

*SEQUENTIAL SITTING UP,
HEAD AND SPINE, LEG UP AND STRETCH

I Should Have Known Better
Two of Us
Here Comes the Sun
Helter Skelter
Back in the USSR
Dear Prudence
Glass Onion
When I'm Sixty-four
Honey Don't
Eleanor Rigby
Rock and Roll Music
Ob-la-di, Ob-la-da
Honey Pie
Magical Mystery Tour

*KNEES TO CHEST

Hey Jude
Maxwell's Silver Hammer
Here Comes the Sun
Honey Pie
Honey Don't

*FLEX EXTEND

One After 909
For You Blue
Maxwell's Silver Hammer
Rock and Roll Music
Magical Mystery Tour
Flying

*BREATHE IN ON HANDS AND KNEES

Old Brown Shoe
For You Blue
Back in the USSR
Don't Pass Me By
Honey Pie
Honey Don't
Rock and Roll Music
Magical Mystery Tour

STRETCH, SIT, PUSH THROUGH, AND SIT

Get Back
Glass Onion
Little Piggies
Blackbird
Don't Pass Me By
Honey Pie

SIT, PUSH, SIT, ROLL

Blackbird
Two of Us
Honey Pie
Don't Pass Me By
She Said She Said
Lovely Rita

ARCH AND A

Mean Mr. Mustard
Back in the USSR
Little Piggies
Octopus' Garden
Don't Pass Me By
Lovely Rita

BOUNCE AND UP

Glass Onion

Honey Pie
For You Blue
You Won't See Me
Kansas City

*FOOT SERIES

I Should Have Known Better
Rain
Maxwell's Silver Hammer
Yellow Submarine

JUMPS

Mean Mr. Mustard
Little Piggies
Why Don't We Do It in the Road (½ time)
Glass Onion
Everybody's Got Something to Hide 'Cept for Me and My Monkey
Blackbird
Lady Madonna
Rain
Flying
The Word
Kansas City
Fixing a Hole

**THE STANDARD GROUP
(USEFUL SELECTIONS)**

Honey Pie
Everybody's Got Something to Hide 'Cept for Me and My Monkey
Birthday
Blackbird
While My Guitar Gently Weeps
The Word
Wait
Kansas City
You Won't See Me
Baby You Can Drive My Car
I Want to Tell You

Love You Too

Yellow Submarine

Taxman

What You're Doing

Getting Better

When I'm Sixty-four

Sgt. Pepper's Lonely Hearts Club Band

Your Mother Should Know

Penny Lane

Baby You're a Rich Man

WHERE TO FIND THE MUSIC—ALBUMS*

1. *Let It Be:*
   Two of Us
   For You Blue
   Get Back

2. *Abbey Road:*
   Come Together
   Maxwell's Silver Hammer
   Octopus' Garden
   Here Comes the Sun
   Polythene Pam

3. *White Album:*
   Everybody's Got Something to Hide 'Cept For Me and My Monkey
   Cry Baby Cry
   Back in the USSR
   Dear Prudence
   Glass Onion
   Ob-la-di, Ob-la-da
   While My Guitar Gently Weeps
   Blackbird
   Piggies
   Why Don't We Do It in the Road
   Yer Blues
   Helter Skelter
   Honey Pie
   Savoy Truffle

4. *Hey Jude:*
   Can't Buy Me Love
   I Should Have Known Better

*All Beatles albums are carried by Capitol Records (Hollywood and Vine Streets, Hollywood, Calif. 90028).

Paperback Writer
Lady Madonna
Hey Jude
Ballad of John and Yoko

5. *Magical Mystery Tour:*
Magical Mystery Tour
Flying
Your Mother Should Know
Penny Lane

6. *Sgt. Pepper's Lonely Hearts Club Band:*
Getting Better
Sgt. Pepper's Lonely Hearts Club Band
When I'm Sixty-four
Lovely Rita
A Little Help from My Friends

7. *Revolver:*
Taxman
Eleanor Rigby
Yellow Submarine
I Want to Tell You

8. *Rubber Soul:*
Drive My Car
You Won't See Me
The Word
What Goes On
Wait
Run for your Life
If I Needed Someone

9. *Beatles For Sale:*
No Reply
I'm a Loser
Rock and Roll Music
Kansas City
Words of Love

10. *Yellow Submarine:*
Hey Bulldog
Yellow Submarine

I have also compiled a discography (that appears at the end of the book) of some of the more wealthy sources of warmup music that, depending on taste, availability, and applicability, one could look to for material. It is not an exhaustive listing, just a few suggestions that should aid in the easy acquisition of music conducive to the task. Keep in mind that there is music from many sources that *can* work for you (including classical, rock, movie scores, soul, jazz, folk, blues, country western, pop, exercise records, and so on). These are some of the most helpful I have found for the majority of my students. It is a constant effort to continually update my music files, and every day new groups and sounds come on the market that are appealing and applicable.

APPENDIX 4: PROJECTS

There are many ways to apply any given program of instruction, but one of the most valuable is within the context of the classroom. A student can use the techniques described in the classroom either independently, in an actual production, or in some other collaborative effort outside the classroom. In each of these approaches, however, there are obvious drawbacks. Independent application provides no external validation of the work. In actual productions the actor may be literally bombarded with processes, approaches, techniques, and personnel that have no connection to the methods he is trying to work with. Consequently, the actor may have difficulty discerning the value and relationship of the various concepts he is forced to accommodate. In other less formal structures (say a group of friends exploring a given work together), no one can be certain of the accuracy of the communication of the theory, and so any results tend to be problematical. However, in a classroom of students all concentrating on the same problem from the same types of experiential development, using the same conceptual tools, and being assisted or guided by an impartial and committed observer (the teacher), process, progress, and discovery can be observed and participated in by all.

Thus, the class project is an extremely valuable tool for developing understanding and appreciation of the theories and methods being discovered in the class. It is rather like a laboratory experiment in which each class member can experiment in a controlled environment so that the results are immediately verifiable. More importantly, it provides a supportive atmosphere of trust and respect not always found when an actor tries to experiment with tools unfamiliar to his fellows in a production. The class project gives license to each student to use the tools he is learning in the classroom without fear of ridicule from others in the group. Since ridicule, or the threat of it, tends to stifle and invalidate any test the actor may wish to conduct, this is a very important and valuable tool for the movement teacher.

Not all my classes have had the interest or energy to develop a project, and so I do not require one of all classes. But when a group of students *have* applied themselves to a project they are interested in, the results have sometimes been stunning.

The prime consideration, then, is that the class as a whole be interested in working on a project. Once that has been decided, the next step is to find a focus or material for a project. This may be the most difficult step to make, and many of my classes have stumbled at this point. To help with this consideration there are many suggestions I might make, depending on the interests and composition of the class.

The possibilities for projects are enormous, and I will list only a few of the projects proposed or executed by classes in the past.

The Museum

Students as a group go to a selected museum and try through Essence (vocalized and silent) to find the form and essence of the museum and its contents.

The Poem

Students may break into two groups and either deal with two poems or with the same poem independently and endeavor to express the core or essence of the poem through sound and movement. An individual, selected individuals, or the entire group may read parts, or all of the poem before, after, or as the movement occurs. The focus is to attempt to encapsulate and express in sound and movement the reality of the poem.

The Message

A class may desire to deal with some topic or message. One class dealt with the concept of the childish, innocent commercialized Saturday morning fare provided on the TV of the late 1950s as contrasted with the chilling spector of the frequent nuclear war air-raid drills. It ended with the entire group huddled in a circle producing an unending wail of the air-raid siren in unison, trailing off until only one, then none, of the unmoving participants was vocalizing the sound, so similar to a child's wail.

The Concert

Students attend a concert and, perhaps using a recording of some of the music played there, attempt to capture the sights and sounds, emotions, and so on, of the people, orchestra, or band, complete from arrival at the theatre to the intermissions and the final movements after the performance to departure. Space, time, energy, animal essences (for people, instruments, or orchestrations), and other elements could provide quite a rewarding exercise.

The Happening

This could be anything from a party, to a funeral; from a circus, to a battle; from a college football game (complete with half-time) to a delivery room; and so forth. Any meeting of people can provide excellent material requiring creative application of this theory.

The Script

This is the broadest category, and the one most frequently used. It is also the most time consuming and, perhaps, ambitious of undertakings. Sources for scripts are limited only by library facilities, time, and interest. There is Reader's Theatre, Experimental Theatre, Classical Theatre, Children's Theatre, and so on. There are Radio Dramas, Film Scripts, Television Dramas and Theatre (that is, *Playhouse 90* and so forth). The focus in each of these, insofar as the project is concerned, is generally the same as in any project: Attempt to encapsulate and express, in sound and movement, the reality of the work being considered, using the techniques being learned in the classroom.

A BRIEF LIST

The following is a *brief* list of possible projects, some of which have been used in my classrooms in the past. Work on them was done in special in-class laboratory sessions, outside class, some in conjunction with speech and acting teachers, others with only a respected class member as director, but most with a combination of directors and much independent initiative. The point is that each class will pursue and produce whatever they will produce in a manner totally unique to them, and the teacher's responsibility is to provide as little control, guidance, and discipline, and as much support and class time as possible. The rest is up to the class.

The Poem

1. *Transformations* by Anne Sexton; Houghton Mifflin Company; Boston. (use selected poems)
2. *All My Pretty Ones* by Anne Sexton; Houghton Mifflin Company; Boston; 1961. (use selected poems)
3. *Leaves of Grass* by Walt Whitman. (use selected poems)
4. *Knots* by R. D. Laing; Pantheon Books, a Division of Random House, New York, 1970. (use selected readings)

The Play

1. *The Serpent* by Jean-Claude van Itallie; Atheneum, New York, 1969.
2. *Alice In Wonderland, the Forming of a Company and the Making of a Play.* Merlin House. Distributed in U.S. by E. P. Dutton, Inc., New York, 1973 by Rabbit Hole, Inc.
3. *Terminal;* A Collective Work Created by the Open Theater Ensemble; Co-directed by Joseph Chaikin and Roberta Sklar; Scripts, Volume 1, Number 1, November 1971, New York. Shakespeare Festival Public Theater.*
4. *Collision Course: 17 Brief Plays.* Compiled by Edward Parone, Random House, New York, 1968.

As you can see, I tend to favor less formal theatrical genres in connection with the class project. Although any script can be analyzed and explored using the tools described in this book (particularly Essence Work), works more of the environmental and experimental theatre mold tend to guide students away from the sometimes stultifying assumptions about how a certain type of play should be presented, interpreted, and performed. Also, since most students have not seen one of these productions, the preconceptions about character, message, and method are simply avoided.

FINAL WORD

The class project can be an excellent tool for uniting the three primary disciplines of actor training: acting, voice, and movement. In a conservatory situation in which the students in one class are receiving simultaneous and complementary instruction from teachers collaborating in the other disciplines, students may receive special advisory assistance from those teachers (based, of course, on the discretion of the movement teachers and the convenience of the other teachers' time and desire). Where such a close collaboration of specialists exists, the results can be extremely fruitful for all concerned. Even when this is not the case, however, the class project can help actors cement their understanding, awaken creativity, inspire new growth, and fuse the separate disciplines into a single cohesive and creative tool.

---

*Terminal is only one of many fine scripts included in the fine series collated and published in the unfortunately short-lived monthly series entitled SCRIPTS. Some of the scripts contained in the series, such as "The Basic Training of Pavlo Hummel" by David Rabe and "The Rock Garden" by Sam Shepard, can be found in other publications, but other fine scripts suitable for class projects contained in these publications are not so easily accessible.

BIBLIOGRAPHY

ARDREY, ROBERT. *The Territorial Imperative*. New York: Atheneum, 1966.

ARTAUD, ANTONIN. *The Theatre and Its Double*. Translated by Mary Caroline Richards. New York: Grove Press, Inc., 1958.

BARKER, CLIVE. *Theatre Games*. New York: Drama Book Specialists, 1977.

BENEDETTI, ROBERT L. *The Actor at Work*. Englewood Cliffs, N. J.: Prentice-Hall, Inc., 1976.

————. *Seeming, Being, and Becoming*. New York: Drama Book Specialists, 1976.

BENTLEY, ERIC. *In Search of Theatre*. New York: Vintage Books, 1957.

BIRDWHISTELL, RAY L. *Kinesics and Context*. Philadelphia: University of Pennsylvania Press, 1970.

————. "Background to Kinesics." *ETC: A Review of General Semantics*, XIII; No. 2 (Autumn 1955), 10–18.

CHEKOV, MICHAEL. *To the Actor: On the Technique of Acting*. New York: Harper & Row, 1953.

COLE, TOBY. *Acting: A Handbook of the Stanislavski Method*. New York: Crown Publishers, Inc., 1960.

DARWIN, CHARLES. *The Expression of the Emotions in Man and Animals.* Chicago: University of Chicago Press, 1965.

FAST, JULIUS. *Body Language.* New York: M. Evans & Lippincott, 1970.

GROTOWSKI, JERZY. *Towards a Poor Theatre.* New York: Simon and Schuster, 1968.

GUNTHER, BERNARD. *Sense Relaxation Below Your Mind.* New York: Collier Books, 1968.

HAGEN, UTA, AND HASKEL, FRANKEL. *Respect for Acting.* New York: MacMillan, 1973.

HALL, EDWARD T. *The Hidden Dimension.* New York: Doubleday & Co., Inc., 1966.

HENDERSON, HAROLD G. *An Introduction to Haiku.* New York: Anchor, 1958.

HODGE, DAVID G. "On Acting the Role of Scapino in *Scapino!*" A Monograph in Theatre Arts for Master of Fine Arts Degree in Acting. Pennsylvania State University, August 1977.

JOHNSON, ALBERT, AND JOHNSON, BERTHA. *Drama for Classroom and Stage.* New York: A. S. Barnes & Co., 1969.

LABAN, RUDOLF. *Modern Educational Dance,* 2nd ed. revised by Lisa Ullmann. New York: Frederick A. Praeger, 1968.

_____. *The Mastery of Movement.* 2nd ed., revised and enlarged by Lisa Ullmann. New York: Drama Book Specialists, 1967.

LANGER, SUSANNE K. *Feeling and Form.* New York: Charles Scribners' Sons, 1953.

LICHTENBERG, GEORG CHRISTOPH. *A Reasonable Rebel.* Translated from the German by Bernard Smith. London: Ruskin House, 1960.

_____. *The Lichtenberg Reader.* Translated, edited, and introduced by Franz H. Mautner and Henry Hatfield. Boston: Beacon Press, 1959.

McGAW, CHARLES. *Acting is Believing.* New York: Holt, Rinehart & Winston, 1966.

MOORE, SONIA. *The Stanislavski System.* New York: The Viking Press, 1965.

OXENFORD, LYN. *Design for Movement, A Textbook on Stage Movement.* New York: Theatre Arts Books, 1952.

SCHUTZ, WILLIAM C. *Joy: Expanding Human Awareness.* New York: Grove Press, Inc., 1967.

SEIDELMAN, ARTHUR A. "Movement and the Actor," *After Dark,* 13, no. 8 (December 1970), pp. 40–41.

SPOLIN, VIOLA. *Improvisation for the Theatre.* Evanston, Illinois: Northwestern University Press, 1963.

STANISLAVSKI, CONSTANTIN. *An Actor Prepares.* Translated by Elizabeth Reynolds Hapgood. New York: Theatre Arts Books, 1959.

_____. *Building a Character.* Translated by Elizabeth Reynolds Hapgood. New York: Theatre Arts Books, 1949.

_____. *Stanislavski Produces Othello.* Translated by Dr. Helen Novack. New York: Theatre Arts Books, 1963.

Webster's New World Dictionary of the American Language, Second College Edition, William Collins and New World Publishing Company, Inc., Cleveland and New York, 1972 and 1970.

WELLWARTH, GEORGE E. *The Theatre of Protest and Paradox.* New York: New York University Press, 1964.

WHITE, EDWIN AND NARGUERITE BATTYE. *Acting and Stage Movement.* New York: Arc Books, Inc., 1965.

ZORA, JOHN W. *The Essential Delsarte.* Metuchen, N. J.: The Scarecrow Press, Inc., 1968.

DISCOGRAPHY

The address of each record company is given on its first appearance.

HERB ALPERT. *Magic Man.* A & M Records, Inc. (P.O. Box 118, Hollywood, Calif. 90028).

————. *Rise.* A & M Records, Inc.

THE COMMODORES. *Greatest Hits.* Motown Record Corp. (6255 Sunset Blvd., Hollywood, Calif. 90028).

————. *Hot on the Tracks.* Motown Record Corp.

————. *Midnight Magic.* Motown Record Corp.

————. *Movin' On.* Motown Record Corp.

THE CRUSADERS. *Free as the Wind.* ABC Records, Inc. (New York, 10019 or Los Angeles, 90048).

————. *Images.* Blue Thumb Records, Inc. (ABC Records, Inc., New York 10019 or Los Angeles 90048).

————. *Southern Comfort.* Blue Thumb Records, Inc.

————. *Street Life.* MCA Records, Inc. (100 Universal City Plaza, Universal City, Calif. 91608).

DEODATO. *Deodato Two.* CTI Records (1 Rockefeller Plaza, New York 10020).

————. *Prelude.* CTI Records.

————. *Very Together.* MCA Records, Inc.

THE DOOBIE BROTHERS. *The Best of the Doobies.* Warner Bros. Records, Inc. (3300 Warner Blvd, Burbank, Calif. 91510).

————. *One Step Closer.* Warner Bros. Records, Inc.

————. *Takin' It to the Streets.* Warner Bros. Records, Inc.

GEORGE DUKE. *Reach For It.* Epic Records (CBS, Inc., 51 W. 52nd St., New York 10019).

————. *Stanley Clarke/George Duke Project.* Epic Records.

EARTH, WIND, AND FIRE. *All 'n All.* Columbia Records (CBS, Inc., 51 W. 52nd St., New York 10019).

————. *I Am.* Columbia Records.

MAYNARD FERGUSON. *Hot.* Columbia Records.

————. *Chameleon.* Columbia Records.

GRAHAM CENTRAL STATION. *The Entertainer.* Warner Bros. Records, Inc.

————. *My Radio Sure Sounds Good to Me.* Warner Bros. Records, Inc.

GRAND FUNK RAILROAD. *Rock 'n Roll Soul.* Capitol Records, Inc. (Hollywood and Vine Sts., Hollywood, Calif. 90028).

————. *Grand Funk Hits.* Capitol Records, Inc.

GRATEFUL DEAD. *Best of Grateful Dead.* Warner Bros. Records, Inc.

————. *History of Grateful Dead.* Warner Bros. Records, Inc.

ISLEY BROTHERS. *The Heat is On.* T-Neck Records, Inc./Distributed by Columbia and Epic Records (51 W. 52nd St., New York 10019).

————. *3 + 3.* T-Neck Records, Inc.

BOB JAMES. *One.* CTI Records.

————. *Two.* CTI Records.

————. *Three.* CTI Records.

————. *Heads.* Columbia Records.

BROTHERS JOHNSON. *Winers.* A & M Records.

QUINCY JONES. *The Dude.* A & M Records.

————. *Roots.* A & M Records.

————. *Sounds ... And Stuff Like That.* A & M Records.

————. *Walking in Space.* CTI Records.

RICKIE LEE JONES. *Danny's All Star Joint.* Warner Bros. Records, Inc.

————. *Rickie Lee Jones.* Warner Bros Records, Inc.

JANIS JOPLIN. *Janis.* Columbia Records.

————. *Pearl.* Columbia Records.

KC AND THE SUNSHINE BAND. *Who Do Ya Love?* T.K. Records (495 SE, Hialeah, Fla. 33010).

RONNIE LAWS. *Fever.* Blue Note Records. (c/o EMI and United Artists, 6920 Sunset Blvd., Hollywood, Calif. 90028).

_____. *Friends and Strangers*. United Artists Music and Records Group, Inc., (6920 Sunset Blvd., Los Angeles,Calif 90028).

RAMSEY LEWIS. *Back to the Roots*. Cadet Records/A GRT Record Group Co. (1301 Ave. of Americas, New York 10019).

_____. *Tequila Mockingbird*. Columbia Records.

LIPPS, INC. *Mouth to Mouth*. Casablanca Records and Film Works, Inc. (8255 Sunset Blvd., Los Angeles, Calif. 90046).

_____. *Pucker Up*. Casablanca Records and Film Works, Inc.

HERBIE MANN. *Discoteque*. Atlantic Recording Corp. (75 Rockefeller Plaza, New York 10019).

_____. *Push, Push*. Embryo Records/Distributed by Cotillion Records (1841 Broadway, New York 10023).

BUDDY MILES. *All the Faces of Buddy Miles*. Columbia Records.

_____. *Them Changes*. Mercury Record Corp. (35 E. Wacker Dr., Chicago 50601).

WALTER MURPHY. *A Fifth of Beethoven*. Private Stock Records, Ltd. (40 W. 57th St., New York 10019).

_____. *Rhapsody in Blue*. Private Stock Records, Ltd.

OHIO PLAYERS. *Greatest Hits*. Westbound Records, Inc./Nationally distributed by Chess and Janus Records (A Division of GRT Corp., 1633 Broadway, New York 10019).

_____. *Honey*. Phonogram, Inc./Distributed by Phonodisc, Inc. (A Polygram Co., 1 IBM Plaza, Chicago 60611).

_____. *Ouch!* Boardwalk Records (c/o CBS, Inc., 51 W. 52nd St., New York 10019).

THE PLAYERS ASSOCIATION. *Born to Dance*. Vanguard Recording Society, Inc. (71 W. 23rd St., New York 10010).

THE POINTER SISTERS. *Energy*. Planet Records (962 N. La Cienega Blvd., Los Angeles 90069).

_____. *So Excited*. Planet Records.

_____. *Steppin'*. Blue Thumb Records, Inc.

TOM SCOTT. *Street Beat*. Columbia Records.

_____. *The Best of Tom Scott*. Columbia Records.

_____. *Tom Cat*. Victrola Records (c/o RCA Records, 1133 Ave. of Americas, New York 10036).

DONNA SUMMERS. *Love is in Control (Finger on the Trigger)*. Geffen Records (c/o Warner Bros. Records, 3300 Warner Blvd., Burbank, Calif. 91510).

_____. *On the Radio: Greatest Hits Volumes I and II*. Casablanca Records and Film Works, Inc.

TAJ MAHAL. *The Natch'l Blues*. Columbia Records.

_____. *Recycling the Blues and Other Related Stuff*. Columbia Records.

GROVER WASHINGTON, JR. *Feels So Good.* Kudu Records (A Division of Creed Taylor, Inc., 36 E. 57th St., New York 10022).

————. *Inner City Blues. Kudu Records.*

————. *Mister Magic.* Kudu Records.

SOUND TRACKS:

All That Jazz. Casablanca Records and Film Works, Inc.

Easy Rider. Dunhill Records, Inc. (A Subsidiary of ABC Records, Inc., 1330 Ave. of Americas, New York 10019).

Grease. MGM Records Corp. (7165 Sunset Blvd., Hollywood, Calif. 90046).

Rocky I, II, and III. United Artists Music and Records Group, Inc.

Saturday Night Fever. RSO Records, Inc. (8335 Sunset Blvd., Los Angeles 90069).

The Wiz. Atlantic Recording Corp.

245